WELL VERSED

Published by Hearing Eye 2009

Hearing Eye
Box 1, 99 Torriano Avenue, London NW5 2RX, UK

ISBN 978-1-905082-42-1

The woodcuts depict workers of the insect world.

The editor wishes to thank Richard Bagley, features editor of the *Morning Star*, David Floyd and Susan Johns for their assistance in producing this book.

Design by Emily Johns
Set in Book Antiqua and Gill
Cover design by Morning Star
Printed by Aldgate Press

Well Versed

An anthology of poems
from the Morning Star

Selected by John Rety

Decorations by Emily Johns

HEARING EYE

Preface

We should all be indebted to the *Morning Star*'s poetry collection, which is full of fun, sadness, cynicism and anger. It is important to understand the close link between art and socialism, for both are international and both speak across the barriers of language and local culture. The poet expresses his or her perception of life in a form that speaks directly to us, whether in rhyme or not, because it escapes the rigid discipline of grammar that is so tightly imposed by our educational system, which can deny us an understanding of what the author really feels and wants to express freely. This collection, so skilfully selected, certainly helps us to see the world through the poet's eyes and share the poet's interpretation of the world as he and she experience it in their hearts, minds and souls.

For many years, I have been fortunate to be sent poems of all kinds written by people of every age. Some come from people who are obviously living under great stress and there are a few regularly who are actually detained and want to be understood and treated as normal, so I always try to reply and thank them for their ideas and talent. And, make no mistake, many of the poets whose work I have read are brilliant in their interpretation of the reality we often miss in our newspapers, with their cold stiff language and limited imagination.

It would be invidious to seek to select those poems in this collection for special mention, but several which I especially liked, I noticed, were written by women. All, in their own way, give a unique word-picture of this challenging and often dangerous world.

Tony Benn

Introduction

The poems in this book are from the first two years of the 'Well Versed' column in the *Morning Star*, from 2006 to early 2008. They are presented in the exact order in which they appeared weekly in the newspaper.

There are many ways to organise an anthology; here it seemed important to use the chronological order. This hints at the selection process that plucked a poem week by week; a poem which consciously or subconsciously resonated with events of the time. Having recently read through all the poems in one sitting, I relived the excitement of choosing them. It was pleasant for me to find little markers of the point in the year with poems for May Day or Christmas . In an understated way the selection has become a record of a feeling of the time. In many instances they echo contemporary worries such as wars and working conditions: anguish at what was happening but with humour to make things bearable. A choice of poems cannot be divorced from one's view of life. Some of these poems shine a light in dark recesses. Some point to the absurdities of life. There is real love, there is real anger, there is biting satire, and there is also celebration when it is called for.

The first poem I chose is by the late Arthur Jacobs and I hope it sets a tone which can be heard through the book — a recurring confident voice, always eloquent, quirky and wise. Most of the contributors are contemporary authors whose thoughts and sentiments I felt needed to be kept in the public's eye. The poems hint at a new age when the ethics which exist behind closed doors might suddenly, as if by quantum leap, take over the public domain.

Each epoch expresses the same basic ideas in its own way and poems may survive for thousands of years. Readers of the future may be sure that the poems in this book were the thoughts of a company of poets talking without guile to their fellows in love and rage. Gone are the artifices or subterfuges that previous ages insisted upon.

It is difficult to tell whether a reader a hundred years hence will regard this selection as many individual voices or as a single common voice. It is not just that our language has changed but the mode of poetry also. I think some poems are written for the daily life of their age, yet some will remain timeless. This is not new. Herbert Read and Bonamy Dobrée, editing the *London Book of English Verse* (from Chaucer to T.S. Eliot) in 1952, had to leave out many poems that were once very popular. In their editorial, referring to the two most popular anthologies, Palgrave's *Golden Treasury* and Quiller-Couch's *Oxford Book of English Verse*, they say, "...in the application of our standard we have rejected nearly half the material offered by Palgrave and Quiller-Couch...[for there has been] some definable barrier, some gauge of appreciation, which has sifted out what in 1860 or 1900 seemed perfect ore." Alas, this applies to 1952 as well.

Many of the contributing poets are also translators. Through their work we are able to reach into the poetry of other peoples and thus remove some of the insularity caused by language barriers. The translations widen the outlook of the collection and show that the concerns here are not parochial but international.

Another pleasure for me on reading through the book was to suddenly come upon lyrics which I could not read, but only sing. It brought a warmth which was quite unexpected and took me back to memories of standing shoulder to shoulder in past assemblies singing with the multitude these rare songs of humanity.

There are not any of my own poems in this collection for I hold that an editor cannot include his own work. But in an introduction I may break my own rules:

The most we can hope for
Is that we might be understood by others
With different understandings to ourselves.

John Rety

Contents

with date of publication in the *Morning Star*

A.C. Jacobs

What Are You Talking About?

Afterwards, as we know,
There are those who virtuously
Declare: We didn't know.

Things happened somewhere else,
Or didn't happen like that,
Or we weren't really told.

Anyway, we had no power
To alter or divert
What did or didn't go on.

It's a familiar sound
To be heard among us now,
The deceiving whine of those
Who participate and know.

Jacques Prévert

Grand Families

Louis I
Louis II
Louis III
Louis IV
Louis V
Louis VI
Louis VII
Louis VIII
Louis IX
Louis X (the Quarrelsome)
Louis XI
Louis XII
Louis XIII
Louis XIV
Louis XV
Louis XVI
Louis XVIII
and nobody, nothing more ...
what's with those people
who can't bloody well even
count up to twenty?

Translation by Sarah Lawson

Anna Robinson

Days Like This

We're running, heads thrown back so we can see
how fast we are, faster than the clouds
(today's windy) and faster than the police
whose cordon we broke through at Waterloo.

There's so many of us and the sun is hanging
so low above York Road and is bouncing itself
off so many windows it has made a long
gold tunnel that none of us could resist.

I have the megaphone. This is not normal.
I'm usually the one with the banner,
wind-surfing to rallies with someone smaller
than me, but not today — today I can see

my long voice spreading out in front
shimmering like a heat haze towards
the bridge where it blends with others
and we look like one, we believe we can fly.

We're heading for Westminster Bridge and later,
after the stand-off and riot (which will begin
when some drift home and the crowd gets smaller
and we're stuck and night's wet-blanket takes

the shine off our skins, just before that woman
from Tottenham - Maria, I think — has her leg
broken by a police horse) will it prove
worth it? We won't get to win this one,

but we ran, heads back, down that road and now
on days like this, in a certain light, I'm weightless.

Beata Duncan

Problem Page

Virginia Woolf is not a pen-name,
the writer married a Woolf.
Use of a pseudonym is unlikely
to stop boyfriend or sister
seeing themselves in your novel.

What a shame Prince Albert
melted on the Christmas tree
and great grandma cried!
Model him in marzipan next time,
it will not harm her gums.

Well done! You have completed
a Dutch landscape puzzle
the Queen found difficult.
Why not write to a lady-in-waiting
and offer to assist Her Majesty
fit the missing bits?

It is not the custom in this country
to ask for doggy bags at parties;
but you could help with the dishes
and sneak goodies into bag
or inner pocket.

Feel free to send me all your problems.

David Floyd

Auntie Gert's Funeral

I was too young
to go to Auntie Gert's funeral
but I'll never forget it

Of course
the church doesn't forgive
those pesky agnostics
who want a last ditch stab at heaven

This vicar in particular
got his revenge
by proceeding to conduct
the entire service
referring to Auntie Gert as Madge

I can't believe
the whole family just sat there
and didn't point it out

If we were Americans
we'd have picked up the coffin
and taken it to an alternative crematorium

After the service
Uncle Mick tried to
smack the vicar in the mouth

I wonder what happened to Madge

Miroslav Jancic

The Birch Grove

On the slopes of Sarajevo
There used to be a placid birch grove
Carpeted by gentle grass and daisies
Where I kissed my first girl
And carved our monograms and
Hearts in the white bark of a birch.

Now there is nothing in the place
Just some empty cans and plastic
Bags, no trace of the birches,
Just the yellow clay furrowed by
Grenades, where young lovers
Made love once upon a time.

Sarah Lawson

Leda

My wings are strong enough to break
A man's leg, you know. I could take
One good swipe with my splendid wing,
One strong stroke would be enough.
He'd be down before he knew a thing
After my solid swan-wing cuff.

A swaggering swan is a sight to see.
As he bragged to Leda about how he
Was so strong, he invaded her private space.
She avoided an attempted peck.
She gazed firmly into his face,
Reached out and wrung his neck.

Perse Peett

On Reading Dylan Thomas in the Pub

The Big Match: The Prince Albert is
swept by an enematic sigh
as the home team barely
fails to score. Juke-box
belting out its tunes. To right
and left loud beery
conversation, clouds of smoke.

In the midst of it all,
me and Dylan Thomas (plus Guinness).
Gripping the book, bracing my feet,
headlong into reading. White-
water rafting on a finely tuned torrent
of words, spray mist of deliberately
disintegrating imagery ......
What other poet's words would
withstand such a barrage of distraction?

This *is* the way to read him.
I feel as though I could
leap up
declaim the poem
and the whole bar will
shoot their fists into the air
and roar
'YYYEEEEESSSSSS!'
then
'Eh?'
before continuing as though
nothing unusual had happened.

Adam Johnson

View From The Monument

Take the three hundred and eleven stairs
(There is no lift), observing as you climb
The nature of the spiral — that it dares
Contest the uniformity of time —

Such eccentricities are why we came:
Wren's Monument — a city's ancient grief
That smoulders in a copper vase of flame,
And Cibber's allegorical relief.

An urban panorama now affords
The true perspective of a vicious age.
The streets we name are nothing more than words
That read in valediction from the page:

Old Jewry, Savage Gardens, Pudding Lane —
Enduring in the wake of enterprise
They cower in the shadow of the crane.
In ranks like weeds the gleaming towers rise:

Encroaching on our vision, they abuse
More than the level aspect of the sky.
Each, from below, the grasping magnate views —
Theirs are our cities, though the cities die.

Paul Birtill

Waiting For My Mother

Fifty-three and totally grey
Wishing to avoid the
young mothers — was always
last to arrive.
I could wait twenty minutes
and then, when the road was clear
in an old coat, looking tired
and perhaps
a little embarrassed
She'd appear.
I was always pleased to
see her — well worth
waiting for was my old mum

Jacques Prévert

A Family Matter

The mother does her knitting
The son makes war
The mother finds this quite natural
And the father, what does the father do?
He does business
His wife does her knitting
His son makes war
He does business
The father finds that quite natural
And the son and the son
What does the son think?
He thinks absolutely nothing
His mother does knitting his father business and he goes to war
When he has finished the war
He will do business with his father
War goes on the mother goes on knitting
The father goes on doing business
The son is killed he no longer goes on
The father and the mother go to the graveyard
The father and mother find that natural
Life continues — life with knitting war business
Business war knitting war
Business business and business
Life with the graveyard

Translation by Sarah Lawson

18

Anthony Edkins

The Nineteenth of August

There's one death we shan't ever forgive:
death of a poet in the sun,
poet of red wounds and kisses
kissed by the blackened mouth of a gun;

there's one death we can't ever forgive:
death of a poet in the sun,
poet of white moon and lilies
lilies and wounds through which the words run;

there are deaths that we'll never forget
deaths of poets in the daylight
poets like dark gypsy riders
riding the wild horses of the night;

there are deaths that we'll never forget
deaths of poets in the daylight
poets of red blood and water,
water's panic and the wind's dawn flight;

there are deaths we'll always remember
through the dead poet's eyes,

eyes that last saw the black mouth of a gun
shouting down Andalucia's bright sun;

under Granada's skies
there are deaths we'll always remember.

Dannie Abse

The Appointment

Since the last place I want to be
is where I'm heading towards
why do I welcome the road signs
which point to that destination?

And since the best I can hope for
is to arrive late, if not later,
why am I pressing down my foot
on the damned accelerator?

David Floyd

Stephanie's Granny Knitted Me A Hat

Stephanie's granny knitted me a hat
this proved that Americans
do not just kill people
they also knit hats

When the people at the university heard the news
they commissioned a survey of politically engaged young people
across the 15 pre-enlargement members of the European Community

The survey found that 83.7% of respondents
believed that the Americans should spend more time
knitting hats and less time killing people

News of the survey results was immediately relayed to the Pentagon
where a spokesman announced that the survey findings
would be carefully considered
but that although the US marines
were trained soldiers
it would be inappropriate to comment
one way or another
on their proficiency with knitting needles

The people at the universities
regarded this as a predictable whitewash
and pointed out that the Palestinian people
would never have a viable state
unless the Americans started knitting them some hats

Stephanie's granny knitted me a hat
she has done her bit

Alan Brownjohn

We are going to see the Rabbit

We are going to see the rabbit,
We are going to see the rabbit.
Which rabbit, people say?
Which rabbit, ask the children?
Which rabbit?
The only rabbit,
The only rabbit in England,
Sitting behind a barbed-wire fence
Under the floodlights, neon lights,
Sodium lights,
Nibbling grass
On the only patch of grass
In England, in England
(Except the grass by the hoardings
Which doesn't count.)
We are going to see the rabbit
And we must be there on time.

First we shall go by escalator,
Then we shall go by underground,
And then we shall go by motorway
And then by helicopterway,
And the last ten yards we shall have to go
On foot.

And now we are going
All the way to see the rabbit,
We are nearly there,
We are longing to see it,
And so is the crowd
Which is here in thousands
With mounted policemen
And big loudspeakers
And bands and banners,
And everyone has come a long way.

But soon we shall see it
Sitting and nibbling
The blades of grass
On the only patch of grass

In — but something has gone wrong!
Why is everyone so angry,
Why is everyone jostling
And slanging and complaining?

The rabbit has gone,
Yes, the rabbit has gone.
He has actually burrowed down into the earth
And made himself a warren, under the earth,
Despite all these people.
And what shall we do?
What can we do?

It is all a pity, you must be disappointed,
Go home and do something else for today,
Go home again, go home for today.
For you cannot hear the rabbit, under the earth,
Remarking rather sadly to himself, by himself,
As he rests in his warren, under the earth:
"It won't be long, they are bound to come,
They are bound to come and find me, even here."

Johannes Kerkhoven

23

Jennifer Johnson

Disconnection and Reconnection

That Thursday had started off so well.
I was going to get to work on time.

Bang! Screams that for months woke me early.

Victorian brick dust and modern peroxide filled our lungs.
We didn't want to breathe this contaminated air
but there was no other. Trapped in that Tube, alongside
a carriage without doors, we talked until breathing got too hard.

Then, the dust cleared a little and we could see those in the dark,
who minutes before might have been reading about love,
now lying on the floor, their bones and muscles exposed
to pictures taken on mobile phones. Half an hour later
doctors shouted "Keep your head still" over and over.

Kept for an hour because "debris had to be removed",
we, sickened, like some animal's innards then spilt towards
the daylight at the end of our darkness,
passed buckled Tube doors and more pieces of glass
than you could imagine: glass like that
we had caught our reflection in so many times before.
We realised body parts were the "debris" they removed.

When we reached Edgware Road, staff handed us
paper towels to wipe off the dirt but there was blood
on the steps and so many with bandaged heads
sitting on the concrete, waiting … I walked on past police,
ambulances, and phoned my boss, shouting above the sirens.

I then walked and walked feeling rootless, disconnected.
Some I'd left behind had families who'd miss them;
I, who live alone, had walked away, found myself lost,
exhausted, but had to keep going somewhere…

I kept busy for a week answering calls of concern, of curiosity.
The two minute silence, though, dissolved my defences.
I couldn't stop crying, wanted to do myself in,
as if the bombings were retribution for my past wrongs.

The police came round for four hours, made me go over
that dark hour. Later, I threw up, wretched for three days,
remembering others who'd tried to kill me,
my mother when I cried beyond her endurance,
someone who, in a row, had tried to strangle me
and muggers who'd once left me for dead.

With each call to the Samaritans I kept rubbing those sores
but needed them to help me connect my present self
to the one out of reach with good memories.

We met up again. Now I use the same Tube line reconnected.

Jo Roach

Shaving

When I'm shaving my father
for the first time, remapping
his face, skin taut against the bone,
the rasp of blade on bristles,
the sag of his neck, stooped shoulders,
the shock of blood, I search for the man
who once worked as a brickie
on the rebuilding of Coventry Cathedral
and the Canvey Island flood defences.
The man in the hospital bed,
after a wall on a job collapsed, breaking his back
as he pushed his mate to safety,
who for months was fed through a straw.
The man who'd received the Last Rites
three times. A man so sickly as a baby,
he was carried on a cushion. The man
who strengthened the foundations of our house
sinking them deep into the London clay.
I study his eyes again, so dark
there is no boundary between iris and pupil.

Raymond Geuss

Invitation

Shall we go to the sand-pits?
Yes, let's go to the sand-pits.

Will the air be fresh and clear
    over the sand-pits?
Depending on the season, the time
    of day, and the weather
the air will be cool, sultry, or mild
    over the sand-pits.

Shall we whistle and get a drink
    at the sand-pits?
Whistling and drinking are *de rigueur*
    at the sand-pits.

Will there be a crowd
    at the sand-pits?
There is almost invariably a crowd
    at the sand-pits.

Shall we take our whips
    to the sand-pits?
In what tree have you parked
    your brain, imbecile?
Without whips what would be the point
    of the sand-pits?

Harry Eyres

Gerald Brenan at Yegen

You put a thousand miles,
two thousand books,
between you and a deaf father, the War,
the fags and philistines of school.

You landed in a village up a mountain,
a people absorbed in their own doings,
uninterested in "where you came from,"
who accepted you and did not moralise.

You could not have asked for more;
distance was what you needed:
looking across the valley towards the sea and Africa
you drank great gulps of the unending air

and freedom. Time opened up
before you and all round,
the snow-fields at your back, larks singing,
your long life's work all ready to begin.

Victor Hugo

Penniless Children

Watch this little one with care,
Filled with God, and great in worth;
Babes, before they come to birth,
Shine above in azure air.

God in bounty gives us this:
They are sent to us on earth,
All his wisdom in their mirth,
All his mercy in their kiss.

We are warmed in their sweet light;
They are cold, and heaven shivers;
They are hungry, Eden suffers;
Happiness was theirs by right.

Men have angels in their power:
Every innocent unfed
Puts on trial the evildoer.
Thunder's rage shall wake the dead:

God, who sent these pretty things
To our den of sleep and shadows,
Sent them down to us with wings,
Finds them wearing rags and tatters!

Translation by Timothy Adès

Gerda Mayer

Unseen

Present met Past,
Said: I am your Future.
But Past walked by
Without look or gesture.

Present then strained
To define Past's nature,
But his sight was too short
To catch every feature.

While Present looked back
Absorbed in the creature,
Future walked by;
Unseen; without gesture.

Janet Simon

Stone

You would reduce this stone to something homely.
Set in the palm of your soft hand,
it rests as if it wouldn't harm a fly.
In your pink fingers, it is a generous stone.
You offer its smooth surface as the best
of possibilities in the best possible of worlds.

You pass this stone to me
with pleasing manners.
You sanction me to hold it
for a few minutes
and to speak uninterrupted
in my own defence.

Your gracious patronage
reduces me to gibberish.
To avoid stuttering
I place this outsized pebble
in my quivering mouth.

Its frigid texture
is cold, impenetrable.
I cannot chew on it
I spit it out.

An angry passer-by
picks up this stone
and hurls it
through your window.
Your creamy skin
turns puce-vermilion,
and as he runs away,
you bolt your doors
and ring for the police.

I bend down and pick up
this stone.
It hasn't changed
its shape or colour.
Its unrelenting stoneness
pleads with me.

I do not understand what force of hatred
makes a man destroy your house,
what speed of terror grabs you to defend it,
but I accept this stone. I hear its silent plea
of guiltless being. It sings to me
in my own ignorance, "I am a stone."
And a stone is a stone is a stone is a stone

Shelah Florey

Out of their hands

I never seem to meet
just a person lately,
they're always trailing
a machine round with them.

It's become so dominant
I feel I ought to greet it first.

Say good morning to the Walkman,
the revving car,
the hedge cutters loud enough
to be demolishing a house.

I shouldn't be surprised
if they answer back quite soon.

Uncivilly of course:
Shut your face,
bugger off —
who said it was a good morning.

Well, I don't blame them really
they must be up to here

with those feeble appendages
hanging on to them.
They want to find themselves,
get out into the world

set up on their own —
be independent.

And the way it's going
it won't be long before they are —
ready to switch off anyone
getting in their way.

Nazim Hikmet

From **Poems to Piraye**
– written between 9 and 10 at nights in prison

23rd September 1945

What is she doing now, at this moment, right now?
Is she at home, or out working,
resting, or on her feet?
She might be lifting her arm,
O, my rose, that movement of your white, firm wrist
strips you so naked...

What is she doing now, at this moment, right now?
Perhaps she's stroking a kitten on her lap,
perhaps she's walking, about to take a step:
those darling, dear ballerina feet
that always bring joy to me on my black days...

What is she thinking about, could it be about me?
Or perhaps about the white beans taking so long to cook,
or why most of humanity is so unhappy?
What is she thinking about now, at this moment, right now?

24th September 1945

The best sea: has yet to be crossed.
The best child: has yet to be born.
The best days: have yet to be lived;
and the best word that I wanted to say to you
is the word that I have not yet said.

25th September 1945

It's nine o'clock.
The bell's gone in the compound.
They'll be shutting the cell doors soon...
This time I've been inside quite a time:
eight years.
Living is work and hope, my darling.
Living, like loving you, is serious work.

26th September 1945

They made prisoners of us, and threw us into jail:
me inside the walls,
you outside the walls.
Ours is small business;
but the worst thing is,
consciously or unconsciously
to have one's soul a prisoner.
Most people are in this situation,
honourable, hard-working people,
worthy of being loved as I love you...

Translation by Richard McKane

Johannes Kerkhoven

Scrabble

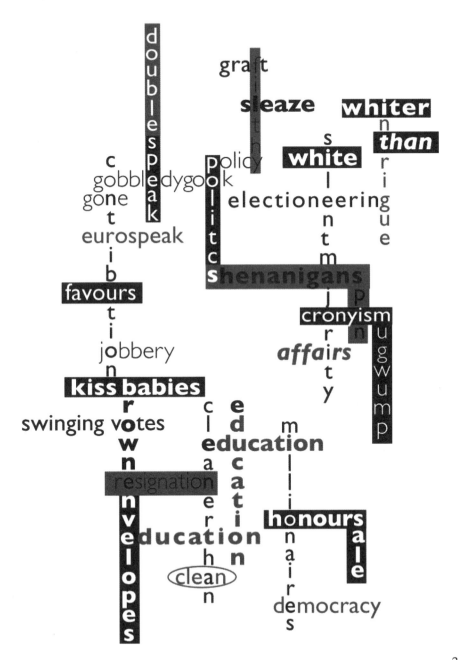

Paul Birtill

Keeping Watch

There is a history of insanity
in that family going back three
generations and they watch each
other like hawks for signs.
They are over-controlled in that house
impulsive behaviour is non-existent.
I stayed there once and nobody
laughed shouted sang cried or
did anything emotional they just
watched — they watched each other
like hawks for signs and
one said as I was leaving,
"It's in our genes you know..."

Mimi Khalvati

Come Close

Think how beautiful we were to start with,
clear as glass. How impossible to part with,
stillness was a rope we tangled round
our mothers' hearts. In sleep we made no sound

Come close the flower says and we come close,
close enough to lift, cup and smell the rose,
breathe in a perfume deep enough to find
language for it, and finding none, unwind

the rope back to a time before we knew
what we know now. When every word was true
and roses smelt divine. What went wrong?
Come closer still, close as the day is long.

Like a rose we slept in the morning sun.
Each vein a small blue river, each eyelash shone.

Peter Phillips

American Immigration

At passport control, Los Angeles Airport,
I showed a bar of Cadbury's Fruit and Nut.

The immigration officer seemed perplexed
and asked again.

This time, after much fumbling,
I gave him a Crunchie bar and a smile.

My wife (who hates any embarrassment)
intervened, apologising for my English humour.

Instead of being sent to the back of the queue
as I expected, I was arrested.

So I took out a Hershey bar and stamped on it.
I'm writing this in prison. Please send more chocolate.

Donald Gardner

I Like my Heron

Dissonant dinosaur of a bird,
claws gingerly stepping along
the corrugated roof of the city farm
he's made his home.

(So he can steal the rabbits' breakfast?)

Closest bird to prehistory,
knobbly knees and straight-out flight,
his shriek cuts the sky like a piece of chalk,
saying:

"So many fish I've had,
I am what I eat.
I can swim the sky."

Now standing erect,
tall and bony,
head turned 180 degrees,

looks like some non-violent philosopher,
if you're not a fish.

Meanwhile a 20-yard long, 12-wheeled articulated tyrannosaurus
has just turned the corner
heading towards the building site opposite,
riding the wrong way down our one-way evolutionary street.

Cars get the hell out of here!
Dogs scram!
No more parking
or barking!

The Amsterdam heron,
symbol of restraint in meditation,
rules my roost.
That's my bird!

Paul Birtill

The Shed

I watched the new tenant
pull down the old shed on Sunday afternoon
and remembered the day it was first
erected, some twenty years ago.
It took half an hour to dismantle
yet had taken the Gunnings' two
sons, Francis and Arthur, most of
an afternoon to build. Their parents
who were on holiday at the time
had been pestering them to put one
up for months, and I think it was
meant as a surprise. When they
had finished they began to argue
and then fight. I shouted
at them both to stop as they rolled around
the lawn exchanging blows and screaming
at one another, but they took no notice.
Then Arthur grabbed a hammer and walloped
Francis several times over the head with it
— he later died in hospital. The Gunnings
returned home the next day to discover they'd
gained a shed and lost a son.

Hylda Sims

Left Rites

When mum, who never quit the Party,
died, the Red Army turned up.
Her Co-op Bentley, English as boot black
trailing limos, slowed through Norwood Cemetery
where Mrs Beeton's bones are stocked
and gothic piety has run to fruit

They stood, peaks, epaulettes, a host
of scarlet stars, flanked by cherubs
epitaphs, cracked angels. Rolling down
the limo glass, I winked, a Cossack,
shamefaced, flushing, dived
behind the BBC pantechnicon

By the chapel, Zils purred. Inside, a comrade
spoke, her casket slid, her anthem rang
and the last fight... The verger, not one of us,
switched off our tape too soon, before
the Internationale unites
the human race, but sure as the sky

dawns rosy over Dulwich, she watched — lights,
rolling, take thirteen — the Beeb shoot *Stalin*
and chortled home with us to bourgeois tea
where, tossing down vodka, clenching our fists
we drank to Trotsky, Lenin, Marx, mother's jokes

Eve Pearce

Whose Child?

Whose child is this, lying by the roadside?
Is it Arab or Israeli?
Lebanese or Iranian?
Palestinian — Iraqi?
Dead or alive?
Is it a Zionist zealot —
a member of Hezbollah?

This child has not yet learnt
there is no God but Allah.
He has no use for an eye for an eye,
a tooth for a tooth.
Whose child is this?

For unto us a child is born.

When he grows up will he attain paradise
in an instant? Will the virgins be waiting?
Meanwhile he has no mother to suckle him —
to be proud when he straps on the martyr's belt.

For unto us a son is given.
A son — is given — unto us.

Whose child is this?

Wanda Barford

"Yes, Madam"

"Fetch your blanket,"
she said to the houseboy,
"and sleep in the kitchen
till the boss comes home."
"Yes, madam," he replied.

The Mau Mau
was spoken of
at bridge and tea parties.
Father would be late back
from his Masonic lodge.

Uneasy, she asked the boy:
"If your brothers
in the Freedom Movement
told you to kill me,
you wouldn't do it, would you?"

"Yes, madam," he replied.

June English

Thanksgiving, October 1970

You at Whiffen Spit, on the seaward side,
where the Cascade mountains rise
in sheeted skies, like the demented
ghosts of wedding cakes, where hawks
and turkey vultures flay the air.

Too quiet, our children's play
in this graveyard of the sea. Pensive,
they sift the bleached bones of cuttlefish
and conch, find a calcified starfish,
ask me why it doesn't swim.

You move to the harbour side, examine
sheltered rock pools where small fish
dart and hide in seaweed gardens,
find a sea anemone, a pulsating cell, red
as a woman's vulva, and poke it with a stick.

Later, in the shell called home,
you strip me, tie me, camera poised,
kneel between my quiveringknees,
thrust screwdrivers into my womb,
skewer the woman from the girl.

Leah Fritz

Brecht

Brecht, where are you when we need you now?
They're forcing things down our throats.
Genetically modified mad cows,
germs without antidotes.
And our voices are stilled with prosperity
or hopelessness, or both.
Brecht, when that Wall came down in Germany
we breathed a sigh. At last
we thought, the whole world's free!
But all that was free were the crooks. And I am past
the stage of euphemism. Where
are your daughters, where your sons, to blast
away the dust-motes of despair?
To sing the true note, with genius and gall
that free isn't free till it's fair?
Why didn't we see the wall behind the Wall?

Alan Brownjohn

Union Man

His liquid lunches will not have unhoned
This lean man, upright at the bar
With the minutes of the last executive
In a thick buff wallet, listening precisely
And working through strategies. His brow
Is furrowed with niceties, his craft
Is the unravelment and intertwining
Of clauses in tense agreements. He gives
A week-end course in grievance and recompense,
And Monday, drives via home to all his high
Cabinets of cases, when the telephone
Clangs to the carpet as he stretches out far to a file
On a distant shelf, and listening precisely.
In a city where minds are slabbed with gold,
He builds a sheltering-wall of brick; and how
The commonwealth doth need such justices.

44

Maureen Duffy

Naming
for Adam Johnson

There's always another "last Romantic".
Playing the tape you made me years now ago
into this cold grey summer evening of your dying
with Jessye Norman blackly in Strauss,
one of life's better ironies
and Mahler's boys jumping out of the bushes
I understand you had to die young
getting better all the time as Keats
or Owen or even the dear bright faker
Tom Chatterton elegantly slumped
under his garret window, a dangling hand
languid on the floor.

I'm writing in anger of course, at loss, at waste
shedding hard dry-point tears on this page
for a poet fucked to death, not just
by the moth hands on the heath, magicked
under lamplight and the kissing, keening
canopy of leaves, but by the dogstar
at your birth that spelled a constant seeking
whose end you already half knew could only come
in words spilt on the paper sheets
not the soft touch, hard thrust of brief encounters.

I look up that Stalybridge you had to come from
on the edge of city and moor, a lot like Hampstead.
The hedges are veiled with lace of cow parsley
and deathly May blossom for the marriage
of another virgin Spring you can't see.
No shabby old skin overcoat for you.
There in the bed you were thirteen again
your flesh like a child's pearled and smooth
your face gone back to tender jailbait.
In these last few minutes before the cruel
bell rang you in, you honed the art of naming
things and places and taught us with your passion
against the grain, how poetry still matters.

John Heath-Stubbs

Chimaeras — Their Origins

Celestial Sophia sat enthroned
Within the darkness of the Unknown God.
It was the Sixth Day, and she was busy
Sewing and snipping, and cutting out patterns —
Patterns of quadrupeds, beasts and cattle,
Serpents, alligators, human beings.
The selfish genes, her servants,
And the environmental factors
Stood by to work those patterns out.
But there were remnants which they rejected —
Heads and tails, wings and limbs and claws.
They drifted into the trashcan of the Cosmos.

Beelzebub, Lucifer and their confederates
The Rebel Angels had all been swept there
Some days previously. The babyish devils
Delighted in those anonymous fragments,
Creating chimaeras, beasts discordantly made up
Of incompatible parts — as hippogriffs,
Sphinxes, bucentaurs, tragopans,
Gorgons and cockatrices.
But the devils soon matured
And got engrossed in a more adult project —
The engineering of the Fall of Man.

Discarded now, the chimaeras
Still bombinated in their vacuum.

Katherine Gallagher

The Last War

There was only one war, and it was finishing
any day soon. Ears keyed to the wireless,
we waited. Then the news: *Japan bombed*,
gigantic clouds curling, skies burnt scarlet —
total destruction...

We've won, we've won, a conga chant
round the schoolground, beating tins, sticks:
our teacher joining in — flags, jumbled cries —
uncles and cousins coming back. The war over.

Hiroshima, Nagasaki — ghost towns now.
Over two hundred thousand people
ghosts too. We couldn't imagine it.

The bomb entered our conversation,
a stranger who refused to leave.
Only years on did we become aware
of the pit of ash beneath our tongues.

Arthur Clegg

Human

I spared it with the hoe
that tiny plant
wind-borne
or bird-dropped,
primrose, I thought

It strove for life
for food, for sun
pushing out roots
and leaves.
A cowslip now
glorious in spring.

Humans strive
for food, for warmth
striving together for better
better than nature gives:
that sharpened flint
the pointed stick
words
the dance

Our human quality
to strive
for better
a better world

Jude Rosen

Remnants

All the schmutters of my childhood:
Verdrei dem kop, Schlug dem kop
im wand irein — the ragged refrains
between the washing and the ironing,
the non-stop running round.
Nicht gefiddled — so the music wasn't played…
Nicht getroffen — so what? The tatters

of the language passed down remain
threadbare cast-offs, slightly stiffened
by German at school. Then our parents
had to leave the room to keep
their secrets intact. *Maschugge zum tod*
— mad unto death — or "more out than in"
as my mother would say…

Yiddish as a second skin has been
replaced by a cloak of *Yiddischkeit,*
the line is running out…
Words dropped on untended ground
could not root… so the land has run dry.
Gut morgen raytach trug ich
— Good morning, I am carrying radish —
has become a real non sequitur.

Paul Birtill

Let's Hear it for the Mentally Ill!

They don't push you around
or sleep with your wife.
They don't enter politics
or refuse you a smoke.
Let's hear it for the mentally ill!

They don't have big egos
or drive fast cars.
They don't go jogging
or play five a side.
Let's hear it for the mentally ill!

They don't travel abroad
or dress up smart.
They don't become famous
or compete in any way.
Let's hear it for the mentally ill!

They don't attend weddings
or have much fun.
They don't have children
or live that long.
Let's hear it for the mentally ill!

Adrian Mitchell

The Doorbell

I was in bed, the silvery light of dawn
blessing our quiet suburban street,
when the window darkened,
and the doorbell rang.

Pushed my face deep in the pillow.
But the doorbell kept ringing
and there was another sound,
like the crying of a siren,
so I slopped downstairs
unbolted, unlocked, unchained
and opened the front door.

There, on the doorstep, stood the War.
It filled my front garden,
filled the entire street
and blotted out the sky.
It was human and monstrous,
shapeless, enormous,
with torn and poisoned skin which bled
streams of yellow, red and black.

The War had many millions of heads
both dead and half-alive,
some moaning, some screaming,
some whispering,
in every language known on earth,
goodbye, my love.

The War had many millions of eyes
and all wept tears of molten steel.
Then the War spoke to me
in a voice of bombs and gunfire:
I am your War.
Can I come in?

Gillian Spragg

Sans merci

It was a small flame
But notwithstanding
Hot enough to sear the
Spot where charity
Could have — where it
Should have — rooted, with the gentle aim
Of nurturing humanity.

Small, barely a glow
Yet still with heat intense
Sufficient to scorch to a
Cinder the sacred place where
Kinder feelings
Formerly — where they
Normally — would blossom sweet and grow
To comforting maturity.

The site is arid,
Parched and desert,
Wasted into dust.

Fled are the well-springs
That might have given ease,
And no bird sings.

A sounding brass, the sun hangs hollow
In a burnished, brilliant sky
And hatred rings.

Paul Summers

Judgement Day

it's baking hot. we regret wearing coats.
from the slit top-deck window of a 39 bus
a skinny, ginger kid in a kappa tracksuit
shouts paki cunts at two old arabs.
the gobful of pepsi he spits at them
blows back, narrowly misses our bags.
he mutters sorry when i stare. there is
a crusty glue-sore on his bottom lip &
his skin is overly pink, like a wax crayon.
his two fat mates obviously think he's cool.
they laugh their tits off at his every move,
taking tokes off the regal kingsize they'd
bummed just then from the pipe-cleaner
woman with bleached blonde hair. they
smoke it like a spliff, sucking 'til their
cheeks collapse & blowing mis-shaped
smoke-rings over our heads. they look
like orang-utangs, especially the ginger one.

David Floyd

The Dead Swan at the Bus Stop

There was a dead swan
at the bus stop this morning
and everyone was scared because you never know
you never know with dead swans

A small lady with a shopping trolley said
"Stand back, stand back, don't touch it
it's a dead swan, it's a dead swan"

When the bus arrived
the small lady with the shopping trolley
jumped on, pointed and shouted
"Look, look, it's a dead swan
it's a dead swan"

The driver got on his radio
and told the people at the other end
to call the fire brigade
because there was a dead swan
at the bus stop

The fire brigade said
they would only come if
the swan was on fire
so the small lady with the shopping trolley
went home and got some paraffin
and poured it over the swan,
the driver lent her his lighter

When the fire brigade arrived
The small lady with the shopping trolley
shouted "Look, look, it's a dead swan
it's a dead swan
it's on fire"

When I got home
my flatmate told me
that she had a dead fox
hanging in her wardrobe

Adrian Mitchell

Dust and Ashes

The Cedars of Lebanon have been stripped of their bark,
cut down to the sap, hacked down to the roots.
Now they are ashes floating over blackened villages.

Israel has locked herself in the bathroom
and is slowly cutting her own throat.

England is hunting down insurgents in Iraq
and terrorists in London,
while selling weapons to anyone who wants to kill.

The USA arms the world at an enormous profit
under the trading name of Shock and Awe.
Washington is the new Rome
whose rulers plan the domination of the world.

What if the weird Barbarians resist?
Bomb them to dust and ashes.
Before we're through
the whole world of Aliens
will become a desert.

Yes the building, the cedars, the animals
and the people will be one dust storm,
a nuclear dust storm swirling round the world.

And when all the men and women and children are dead
in Dubai, Chicago, Beijing, Sydney, Rio de Janeiro and Paris –
when they are all dead
and all the animals
and all the trees
and all the birds
and all the insects —
their ashes will fly in their hot agony
and descend upon the waters,
and the poison ashes will murder the oceans
and all life will be wiped out —
goodbye, my love.

Jean Cassou

Sonnet XXII

The workers in all lands eternally
die. Workers' blood goes streaming underfoot.
The workers stumble in the smoke; they cry.
Fire, winter, iron, the wheel, and hunger put
the workers down. In all lands rotting trees,
bare stones, the rusty grilles of hospices,
since time began, the days of wretchedness,
the herd of days bloodied and on their knees...
O God of justice, throned not in the skies,
but in the heart of man, and of his wrath,
will you not spread your wings at last on earth?
Lord of the strong, of force, unveil your eyes!
The wrists are tied, the lips speak not a word,
the chain is very long. The workers, Lord?

Translation by Timothy Adès

Brian Docherty

Armchair Theatre

We've all played the game of
"Where were you on 22 November 1963?"
tried to describe our grief.

How would the Mafia and the FBI,
the patriotic Klansmen, do on that score.
"It's all a matter of perspective, boy."

A united front of the ruling classes
guns and uniforms and a dead hero.

We had ours with Churchill soon enough
the first state funeral on television.
While the English commentary spoke for Britain
I went to the Tally's for icecream and lemonade.

A man lurched out of the 'Hawthorn'
"Deid at last, deid at last,
th' auld bastard's deid at last."

Making it sound like a cry of freedom
one more link in the chain broken.
Was he remembering Tonypandy 1910
when Churchill sent in the troops.

Or Sidney St. where the Home Secretary
turned up with his personal Tommy gun;
the General Strike and the British Gazette
and Churchill's words to the nation.

We are at war.
We must go through with it.
The Strike must be crushed.
These words from an 'A' level textbook
published by Harold Macmillan's old firm.

Richard Dimbleby mentions none of this
as the First Lord of the Admiralty
rides his last gun-carriage through London
surrounded by the Queen's Navee.

Down at Waterloo Station sits Engine 34051
Winston Churchill, Battle of Britain class;
the corpse has his own train
steaming to his final anchorage.

"Haw see this Armchair Theatre, it's garbage,
turn ower tae the White Heather Club."
Almost anything is preferable
provided it speaks in our own tongue.

Paul Birtill

Christmas without Mum

It just wasn't the same
that first Christmas after
her death, everyone felt it
as we ate our dinner totally
subdued and cheerless.

It was the same the year after —
a sombre and slightly embarrassing affair;
until one by one we stopped coming home,
and my dad went to his sister's in Yorkshire.

Eddie S Linden

City of Razors
for the city of Glasgow

Cobbled streets, littered with broken milk bottles,
reeking chimneys and dirty tenement buildings,
walls scrawled with FUCK THE POPE and
blue-lettered words GOD BLESS THE RANGERS.

Old woman at the corner, arms folded, babe in pram,
a drunk man's voice from the other pavement,
And out come the Catholics from evening
confessional;

A woman roars from the upper window
"They're at it again, Maggie!
Five stitches in our Tommie's face, Lizzie!
Eddie's in the Royal wi' a sword in his stomach
and the razor's floating in the River Clyde."

There is roaring in Hope Street,
They're killing in the Carlton,
There's an ambulance in Bridgeton,
And a laddie in the Royal.

Lynn Foote

Ponteland Chicken Factory

The boy sat with his knife
and slashed those chickens north and south

they tumbled down the chutes
and an anointing scream rose from the women, a bagpipe

playing its macabre tune, as the scrowed old ladies
bounced along the assembly line,

hung from hooks, clawed from below
by a plethora of hands and the guts chucked —

the steaming tray carried to a steely table
whilst the birds perambulated the room,

and I dug my cellophaned mitt
into the spirogyra of necks like willies

gizzards green with grit and bile
and livers hot with the bodies they'd come from

Fifteen minutes of this made one woman sick
so we worked shifts —

the chickens still coming in on the mighty loom —
until washed, our hands acid with it (the gloves often off)

they were graded as A's — no bumps or bruises,
or B's — given to the women, the ones that had bled

whilst the C's — rotten even before they were dead —
disappeared.

At break in our eight-hour day for eight quid pay
(a week) we repaired with the women

to the back room where they ate sandwiches
made with the chickens they'd embalmed yesterday

and my friend Heather and me
well we drank the tea and ate bread and cheese

and counted our good fortune on being the girls
advanced to the chicken-grading, where we have remained...

Peter Campbell

Fourth Station

Cricklewood station,
Cricklewood station.
I wait for the five o'clock
With indignation.
It's down to King's Cross
For a conversation
With a man in a bookshop
Creased with perspiration.

I've never seen the colours over west so hard,
Like ripples of blackcurrant on a faded postcard.
No coronas on the floodlights in the marshalling yard,
It's the kind of night God must have used
For passing on the word.

Graffiti on the shelters
On Cricklewood station,
Chalking the genetic code
Of mass imagination.
Putting out the candles
Of a deeper indignation.
Jumping on the five o'clock
For a private assignation.

I've never heard such singing of the voltage in the wire,
Like the suicidal pleadings of a tabernacle choir.
They can keep you out of work, they can't put out the fire.
It's the kind of night God must have used
To push sexual desire.

Graffiti say that God was here
On Cricklewood station.
If I had known it soon enough
I would have booked a conversation
To offer to that great divine
Heartfelt congratulation
For leaving us a night like this
In form of compensation.

I've never seen the moisture on the brick so sheer,
Like earrings that are clinging to a dead man's ear.
There's a cutting kind of silence in this section of the year.
It's the kind of night God must have used
To make his passion clear.

Cricklewood station,
Cricklewood station.
I wait for the five o'clock
With indignation.
It's down to King's Cross
For a brief flirtation
And the evening in the back row
Of a godless generation.

Lucy Hamilton

Saint Francis in Provence

Italian son of a merchant of fine textiles
and originally named Giovanni,
his father, returning after a long while
away in his beloved France, thought why
not rename his baby boy Francesco?
The child loved animals, birds and flowers
— an equal passion being poetry. So
he joined the French (and courtly) troubadours,
learned to speak and sing in Provençal
and before long was composing his own songs.
Some say his Canticles so resemble Rumi
that they've begun to research links among
those teachers of abstinence and poverty.
Others think the Dervishes stole his soul.

When he was thirty, Francis (or Francesco)
decided to try for Syria in the East
and when that failed he set out for Morocco
to help the poor and to learn to pray and fast.
In Egypt he entered the camp of Saracens
and was granted an audience with the Sultan
who was so impressed he gave permission
for Francis to visit the shrines of Palestine.
Like the Sufis (but unlike ordinary Christians),
the rules he gave disciples didn't incline
to the self: he didn't look to his own salvation,
believing it an expression of vanity.
And he always began '*as-salaamu alaykom*'
preferring the music of the Arab welcome.

Bernard Kops

Shalom Bomb

I want a bomb, my own private bomb, my shalom bomb.
I'll test it in the morning, when my son awakes,
hot and stretching, smelling beautiful from sleep. Boom! Boom!

Come my son dance naked in the room.
I'll test it on the landing and wake my neighbours,
the masons and the whores and the students who live downstairs.

Oh I must have a bomb and I'll throw open windows and
count down as I whizz around the living room,
on his bike, with him flying angels on my shoulder;
and my wife dancing in her dressing gown.
I want a happy family bomb, a do-it-yourself bomb.
I'll climb on the roof and ignite it there about noon.
My improved design will gong the world and we'll all eat lunch.

My pretty little bomb will play a daytime lullaby and
thank you bomb for now my son falls fast asleep.
My lover come close, close the curtains, my lovely bomb, my darling.

My naughty bomb. Burst around us, burst between us, burst within us.

Light up the universe, then linger, linger
while the drone of the world recedes.

Shalom bomb.

I want to explode the breasts of my wife,
and wake everyone,
to explode over playgrounds and parks, just as children
come from schools. I want a laughter bomb,
filled with sherbet fountains, licorice allsorts, chocolate kisses, candyfloss,
tinsel and streamers, balloons and fireworks, lucky bags
bubbles and masks and false noses.

I want my bomb to sprinkle the earth with roses.
I want a one-man-band bomb. My own bomb.

My live long and die happy bomb. My die peacefully at old age bomb,
in my own bed bomb.
My Om Mane Padme Hum Bomb. My Tiddly Om Pom Bomb.
My goodnight bomb, my sleeptight bomb,
my see you in the morning bomb.
I want my bomb, my own private bomb, my Shalom bomb.

Stephen Watts

Marginal note in time of war

His name was not written
(Hannah Arendt)

Walter Benjamin took his own
life out of pure exhaustion, walking
into the mountains against love's gravity
up the scarp slope of his melting reason
to where he was abandoned by language.
Huge lethargies in the world glutted him
then stiff blood came, pulsed out in coils.
Who knows where he could have gone to
after that, except that he couldn't go on, burst
by the butchered choice of angel history,
a tremendous shattering tossed across his
face, tiny maggots gobbling on sunlight,
fascisms in the honeys of his friendship.
His name unwritten, nowhere to be seen.
He who was the loveliest among people.
Why did no-one tell him when he lived?
Nothing was left to hold him on the hill.
Angels could not put back insane reason.
Exhaustion killed him, more than terror,
more than despair, or a theology of dirt.
At the end — when the angel of history
called out his name to mock him — he
walked up higher into the blind frontier
and took his own life on a hillside that
looks over the sea: one of the loveliest
places on earth, as Hannah Arendt said,
        and like himself, halfway up
            and halfway down.

Oliver Bernard

Tom leaves the Norfolk and Norwich Hospital and comes back to Kenninghall

On your third morning Tom
you come out of hospital
to live in our street
where we've lived all the time.

Waiting for you was good
it reminded us how much
your mother meant to us.
Though we saw the space
between cup and lip
her hand never shook.
She carried you down to the market place
and back up the hill.
She didn't know when you'd come
but she always smiled about it.
(Waiting for her news
she was always good news.)

Now you come up the hill
on the third day of your life
and there's the big brothers
and a kitten called Sam
and amazing green stuff
grows outside the door
and swifts all summer long
and stars on winter nights.
But for us there's you
to make everything good.

Everything has to be good
not so much by being
changed as illuminated
from time to time.

From time to time we know
people are what matters
trees are for consolation
food is good when you're hungry
faith is for keeping.

(There's your father
I've seen him dead beat
and still smiling
cycling uphill
from a day at the factory.)

I don't say, be a communist:
what I say is be
the kind of man who
is sometimes accused
by those whose lives are mean
and governed by distrust
of being what they call
"some kind of communist."

A.C. Jacobs

Prime of a Statesman

Whatever his real gifts,
                          whatever
Lonely dramas to match the time's need
He enacted,
               the leader lives in adulation
Now.
          The party press is warmed
By the mere thought of him,

The opposition are disgruntled
But lie meshed in his legend,

The people are convinced
They cannot do without him

              And he goes
Bible-quoting,
                  buoyant on history,
So that it seems that government
Is a gift
            for fluent rhetoric.

Erich Fried

Death Certificate

"Because it's all no use
They do as they please anyhow

Because I don't want to get
my fingers burnt again

Because they'll just laugh:
it only needed you!

And why always me?
I'll get no thanks for it

Because nobody can sort this out
One might only make things worse

Because even what's bad
may have some good in it

Because it depends how you look at it
and anyway whom you can trust?

Because that other side too
gets wet when it rains

Because I'd rather leave it
to those more qualified

Because you never know
what you let yourself in for

Because it's a waste of effort
They don't deserve it"

These are the causes of death
to write on our graves

which will not even be dug
if these are the causes

Translation by Georg Rapp

Jeremy Kingston

The Taste of his Hair

His hair always smelled of soot
He didn't smoke
He wasn't even Santa Claus
But whenever I sank my face in his
crisp black hair I would smell this
dry and powdery, aromatic
bliss.
It was a drug for me.
If I start sweeping chimneys for a living he'll be why.
Maybe it was some Korean drug he took, or a dish
at that place where tofu was never off the menu.
I want to think it was simply
essence of him
that I shared for a while
marvelling.
What I do know is that his sweetly
sooty taste
has not stayed in the past
but catches up with me at any time
and may go on doing so till a day or two before
essence of me
(that I shall not smell)
really goes up a chimney.

Paul Birtill

November 22nd London

It never really got light today,
I've seen days like it before
this time of year. But the leaves
they are so beautiful this autumn,
such unusual colours: We should be
grateful to the Victorians, strange
though they were, for planting so many
trees, it must have taken their minds
off sex — poor souls.

Geoffrey Hazard

Portrait

Sweetness shows on his face.
His hands clutch blindly at the stars.
His eyes are political
and ambitious.
He in the tomb of night
writes on the crumbling city walls
the message of escape
in a child's scrawl.
He is like a flower
that prefaces the earth
with a gnarled symbol
of the deepest birth.

Bernard Kops

Whitechapel Library, Aldgate East

How often I went in for warmth and a doze
The newspaper room whilst my world outside froze
And I took out my sardine sandwich feast.
Whitechapel Library, Aldgate East.
And the tramps and the madman and the chattering crone.
The smell of their farts could turn you to stone
But anywhere, anywhere was better than home.

The joy to escape from family and war.
But how can you have dreams?
you'll end up on the floor.
Be like your brothers, what else is life for?

You're lost and you're drifting, settle down, get a job.
Meet a nice Jewish girl, work hard, earn a few bob.
Get married, have kids; a nice home on the never
and save for the future and days of rough weather.

Come back down to earth, there is nothing more.
I listened and nodded, like I knew the score,
and early next morning I crept out the door.

Outside it was pouring.
I was leaving forever.

I was finally, irrevocably done with this scene,
The trap of my world in Stepney Green.
With nowhere to go and nothing to dream.

A loner in love with words, but so lost
I wandered the streets, not counting the cost.

I emerged out of childhood with nowhere to hide
when a door called my name
and pulled me inside.

And being so hungry I fell on the feast.
Whitechapel Library, Aldgate East.

And my brain explodes when I suddenly find
an orchard within for the heart and the mind.
The past was a mirage I'd left far behind.

And I am a locust and I'm at a feast.
Whitechapel Library, Aldgate East.

And Rosenberg also came to get out of the cold
To write poems of fire, but he never grew old.
And here I met Chekov, Tolstoy, Meyerhold.
I entered their words, their dark visions of gold.

The reference library, where my thoughts were to rage.
I ate book after book, page after page.
I scoffed poetry for breakfast and novels for tea.
And plays for my supper. No more poverty.
Welcome young poet, in here you are free
to follow your star to where you should be.

That door of the library was the door into me.

And Lorca and Shelley said "Come to the feast"
Whitechapel Library, Aldgate East.

Martin Green

Marx v Smith

Adam Smith's Wealth of Nations,
Capital's firm foundations;
Next came Marx who saw the rot
Inherent in the building plot.
He knew that wealth created dearth
By robbing those who tilled the earth.
His Communist Manifesto
Made Capitalism, presto!
Apologists stepped to the fore
And Economics became Law.
Let's stand aside and take a look
At a world which reason has forsook.
Socialism says it can
Improve the common lot of man.
Capitalism says: Oh no,
I amass, you forgo.

Liam Maguire

The poem on the back of the door

It seems a long time now
since I wrote that poem,
the poem on the back of the door.
Bored with the usual run
through the type letters,
capital and case, I wrote
a small poem called Compulsion,
and, grinning at my effortless ease
in writing such a trifle,
I gave it to you.

On the back of the door,
among the other notices,
the monthly diaries,
the numerous phone numbers,
you pinned the poem;
the words heavy black
from the new ribbon.

When a phone numbr
or an event needed checking,
you would read my poem.
'You are not so old,'
you'd say, reading the poem
on the door after we
had made love.

Things familiar get ignored.
The door was no longer shut
for lovemaking and you'd check
in your bag and small diary
for phone numbers or meetings.
'I like your poem on the door,'
a visitor remarked one day.
The next day the torn sheet
was flung on my table
with other scraps of my life
and the door opened to
an empty room.

David Floyd

Here I am Sane

So here I am sane

I am a council-sponsored professional
discharging my duty
to make positive small talk
and change the subject

And as we sit on the bench and watch you
spreadeagled on the grass
in a strangely coloured woolly hat
Steve remembers he will
be in Brazil this time next month
and I think back to all the times
I've been singled out as a lunatic

The time when I fidgeted so much
the hairdresser thought I was "a bit funny"

At school when I made crazy faces
to hide my insecurity
and the little kids called me "mental"

When I ran away
from the yappy little dog
and Brendan said I had a fur allergy

There are too many to mention
but they never sent me here
to this demented corner of Tottenham
where agency social workers go to die

What have mad people done to deserve this?
Why do all those right-headed people
who've subjected us to world wars, starvation and

mind-numbing TV dramas starring Ross Kemp
get to live in comfort in Highgate
and hold lengthy discussions on the meaning of modern art?

Surely they should be the ones
condemned to spend their nights
in a desperately normal excuse for a bedroom
next to a traumatised soldier
who shrieks in Greek
and pretends to slit his throat

You say you've read the papers
and the end of the world is coming soon
I say it isn't
it is only Wednesday
and here I am sane

Paul Birtill

Do Not Disturb

If I'd been asleep for a thousand years
and some fool happy couple offered me birth,
and the chance to come back to sad planet earth.

I'd tell them no thanks, because I've been there
before — seen what it's like and don't want
anymore.

Their politics, religion, and evil wars.
The suffering, misery, and unfair laws —
needing drugs and alcohol just to get through.
I don't want another go and be honest, do you?

James Harvey

The Butterfly Counters

They count butterflies that come into range
as each walks along a preordained route
marking the types and how the numbers change.

Once a week, spring and summer, they estrange
themselves from company, and keeping mute
they count the butterflies that come into range,

each one part in a network of exchange
so the local and national compute,
marking the types and how the numbers change,

and if the route starts to feel cold and strange
because the sense one is missing is acute
they count the butterflies that come into range,

with changing land patterns types rearrange,
they can see emerging a substitute
marking the types and how the numbers change,

with a national shortage, on the danger
list, a butterfly becomes a rare fruit,
they count butterflies that come into range
marking the types and how the numbers change.

Dinah Livingstone

May Day

A May morning at Minsmere,
in the bird reserve, many calls
I can't identify — some singing,
some sound more conversational
and the bass is the rhythm of the sea.

Before me in young leaf the May tree
stands frothing with starry blossom,
milky sunlit epiphany:
in admiration hope does not fail.

The tree is thick and squat,
its comfortable shape,
tousled on top,
spikes the hazy blue
now clearing to speedwell.

Its flowering month
opens with that annual outburst
of belief in life before death,
faith leading to insight
of a species as whole-heartedly human
as it is most tranquilly tree.

Of course they want to cancel it.
These bosses despise
workers, makers, seers,
deny their holiday.
Time runs out on earth.
May Day. May Day. May Day...

Jacqueline Gabbitas

An' Each Dot a Bomb

It wa a map framed on't wall, backorra door.
Snided, snided in dots it wa like woodlice
on a strippa rotten timber, loads more
though, an' each dot a bomb and t'size
o' mi right pupil, cos mi left's rate small,
an't' streets wa' thick as t'veins in mi arms.
When I wok up in't neet, I'd been falling,
mi face an' feet wa cold, mi hands warm,
mi stomach an' all. I bent mi 'ead on mi wrist
and it wa mi pulse I could hear like a tattoo,
or like a machine printing; I listened
in't dark to all that iron in mi blood
racing and knew from iron, steel gets med,
and from steel, 's picture wire, 's pin heads.

Robert Ilson

Jack Gaster in Memoriam

Campaigns make headlines; friendship, memories.
Empires felt his wrath; I ate his cake —
Better than whatsoever I could bake —
Offered to me at the impromptu teas
I got when I thought I had come to give.
A dire defeat, in Jack's vicinity,
Became a stepping-stone to victory
And helped not just "Humanity" to live
But me, his guest, who'd wanted to help *him*!
Why am I saying this? You knew him too
And each could say as much. We're here because
He knew us as we knew him. More than whim
Has gathered us to say farewell to who
Was dear for what he did — and what he was!

David Floyd

Self-sufficient

It would probably be possible
to avoid an alien invasion
by shutting the door.

Given the increasing range
of TV programmes now available
with little or no reference
to the schedules

you could easily just
line up everything you want
to watch for the next month

then, as long as you were
well stocked with tinned food
if and when the aliens attacked

you would not need to
concern yourself with
any disruption to
your viewing pleasure

as long as you had your own
generator and access to a
hidden supply of fresh spring water.

You might get found, eventually
but these things have a habit
of blowing over.

Paul Birtill

Hell on Earth

I don't think any First World War poet
would have bothered with a creative
writing course. They learnt their skills
in the trenches ankle-deep in sludge, and
bled their hearts out in No Man's Land.
No-one could teach them how to write,
they were there — saw everything. What else
could they do but write, or go mad?

Paul Celan

Aspen Tree (Espenbaum)

Aspen tree, your leaves gaze white into darkness.
My mother's hair never turned white.

Dandelion, so green is the Ukraine.
My blonde mother did not come home.

Rain cloud, do you linger by the springs?
My quiet mother weeps for everyone.

Round star, you tie the golden bow.
My mother's heart was wounded by lead.

Oaken door, who lifted you from your hinges?
My gentle mother cannot come.

Translation by Vincent Homolka

Martin Green

The Malodorous Isles

A clutch of inhospitable rock
Anchored in south Atlantic seas —
Les Malouines the French dubbed them,
Corrupted by the Spanish to *Las Malvinas*
Taken for the British by one Davis
Whose deed was commemorated
By the bequest of Lord Falkland's name.

The terrain inhospitable
The population sparse
The owners, through a trick
                    of capitalistic circumstance
The Coalite Company.

The profits are small
The life is hard.
The British who have lived here longest
Were disenfranchised by Act of Parliament.

An anachronistic military junta
                    in Argentina
Wrested these islands from a handful of marines.
An anachronistic civilian junta in
                    Downing Street
Retaliated by launching one of the most
                    formidable armadas of all time
To fight over this inhospitable peaty soil
Where no crows thrive.

Sovereignty — what's in a name?
Belonged to no-one, then France, Spain
Then Argentina, then Britain.

Who has sovereignty over the dead?
The dead.

Jeremy Kingston

Paying for the Games

They've chopped the budget at the BFI,
at your local arts centre,
at the publishing house that might have let you read this poem.
But don't worry,
don't upset yourself.
Instead of preserving old films, creating drama,
spreading thought and feeling
someone will be shaving one fifth of a second off the
Mixed Hurdles Freestyle. Oh what glory!
Poets and lovers of poetry
surely you're proud
shout it aloud
there'll always be a Mixed Hurdles Freestyle
so much more precious
so much more vital
than Shakespeare, Goethe and all the sorry rest of them
who probably couldn't run a mile in four-
teen minutes
and never thought it worth trying to.
So look on the bright side,
every cloud has a silver lining
or a gold lining
even a bronze one'll do.
Poetry? Forget it.
When they ask you about metre
it's the hundred and the four hundred they're on about,
the feet in a line
are waiting for the starting pistol,
and the finishing line
is the end of everything that matters.

Rose Ausländer

You are still here (Noch bist du da)

Fling your fear
into the air

Soon
your time will be up
soon
the sky will grow
beneath the grass
your dreams fall
into nowhere

The carnation
still is fragrant
the thrush still sings
you can still love
give words away
you are still here

Be what you are
Give what you have

Translation by Vincent Homolka

Heinrich Heine

Angels

Now I don't believe in heaven,
I'm really a Doubting Thomas,
though religion says we are given
both Rome's and Jerusalem's promise.

But on whether angels are real
I've never had any doubt;
they are creatures of light, ideal:
here on earth they are roaming about.

I merely maintain they are wingless,
dear lady, these entities:
I know there are wingless angels,
I've seen them with my own eyes.

By their lovable soft sweet hands and
their lovable tender glance,
we mortals are rescued and ransomed,
protected from all mischance.

They console us with their mercies,
their grace to us all is extended:
but most to the doubly tormented,
the poet, the writer of verses.

Translation by Timothy Adès

Andrew Bailey

Lodestar, Polestar

in memoriam Peter Redgrove

Although he is now become lodestar, the water
that flooded the village I lived in was him
and still is him, for steeped in his substance
as I climbed the moonlit path from the water-village,
where the moonlight that lit the way was him,
my moondried self stayed redolent of him.

The north star sings: for you he is with me now.

Then I discipled myself to these uncommandments,
tried to find the stars in sunlit skylights, the doors
to dreams that do not leave or let you close them,
to other minds that fan and close like tarot decks;
I still endeavour, master, to be beesize, mothsize,
or so massive that the flesh that carries you can
seethe the dreams of mice from its pores to join
the tiny bestiaries choiring metamorphoses
among the grasses. The north star sings for me.

The stars that fall fall just as rain, and their ashes
dust clouds, making rain of him; the rain
makes plants of him, and so until we share him,
share his light, which holds still to that star
about which other stars, that are, as we are, him, rotate.

Hylda Sims

Rain Dance

In the night it rains
sudden and steady
There has always been rain
Agamemnon knew rain, Charlemagne
walked out in it; chipping at flints
Neanderthals got soaked to the skin
dinosaurs were often drizzled on
the wool of mammoths frequently
glistened and steamed
with rain
Where there's life there's rain
neutral in its blind will to wet
crying its eyes out sightlessly
on house painters and hod-carriers
kite-flyers, fell-walkers
harvest fairs and cricket matches
washing lines and Wimbledon
funeral weepers, rough sleepers, buskers
bus queues, bikers and barbeques
Oh rain, you chorus dancer
cleaner-upper from above
come down, come on down
soften the city litter, throttle the gutters
shine up the concrete and test the roofs
drip off the leaves and polish the cars
Sweep on rain, sweep on
over continents, islands and seas
over taiga, tundra and town
fall on fertilized fields, foam into fast flowing fiords
drench dusty deserts all set about with papery palm-trees
saturate seared savannahs galloped by gnu and wandered by wildebeest
pour on parched prairies munched by buffalo & pounded by cowpuncher
run down rills in rugged rocks to cols caves and crevasses
flood the Thames with its tall ships, tugs and trippers
inundate the Nile with its bulrushes and barges
Zambezi and Limpopo with their crocodile and hippo
your ferny, fronded forests full of slippery snake and gecko

Splash on, rain, splash on
irrigate gardens
raise up reservoirs
deluge drainpipes
sparkle into swimming pools
burble into waterbarrels
ripple into rivers
flash into fountains
cascade into cataracts
whoosh into waterfalls
waste yourself in torrents and streams —
do it all before dawn — and please
don't take my sunshine away

John Brunner

The H-Bomb's Thunder

Don't you hear the H-Bomb's thunder
Echo like the crack of doom?
While they rend the skies asunder,
Fall-out makes the earth a tomb.
Do you want your home to tumble,
Rise in smoke towards the sky?
Will you let your cities crumble,
Will you see your children die?

Tell the leaders of the nations
Make the whole wide world take heed:
Poison from the radiations
Strikes at every race and creed.
Must you put mankind in danger,
Murder folk in distant lands?
Will you bring death to a stranger,
Have his blood upon your hands?

Shall we lay the world in ruin?
Only you can make the choice,
Stop and think of what you're doing,
Join the march and raise your voice.
Time is short: we must be speedy,
We can see the hungry filled,
House the homeless, help the needy,
Shall we blast, or shall we build?

Men and women stand together,
Do not heed the men of war,
Make your minds up, now or never,
Ban the bomb for ever more.

Ewan MacColl

Song of Hiroshima

In the place where our city was destroyed,
Where we buried the ashes of the ones that we loved,
There the green grass grows and the white waving weeds.

> Deadly the harvest of two atom bombs.
> Then brothers and sisters you must watch and take care
> That the third atom bomb never comes.

The sky hangs like a shroud overhead
And the sun's in the cage of the black, lowering cloud.
No birds fly in the leaden sky,

> Deadly the harvest of two atom bombs.
> Then brothers and sisters you must watch and take care
> That the third atom bomb never comes.

Gentle rain gathers poison from the sky
And the fish carry death in the depths of the sea;
Fishing boats are idle, their owners are blind,

> Deadly the harvest of two atom bombs.
> Then, landsmen and seamen you must watch and take care
> That the third atom bomb never comes.

All that men have created with their hands
And their minds, for the glory of the world we live in,
Now it can be smashed, in a moment destroyed,

> Deadly the harvest of two atom bombs.
> Then people of the world, you must watch and take care
> That the third atom bomb never comes.

Adapted from the Japanese song by Koki Kinoshita
'We will never allow another atom bomb to fall'.

90

Paul Birtill

Global warming

It was snowing when I woke
this morning and was sunny
at midday. There was a party
having their Christmas dinner
in the pub and I got stung by
a bloody great bee — All this
in mid-February. I've also
noticed those old guys with
'THE END IS NIGH' signboards
seem a lot more confident
these days — have a certain
spring in their step.

Eddie S. Linden

The Nest

The echo of the burn as it runs yellow
And dark blue slag on the pit surface
Reminded him of his past.
The wheel of life sounded its
Message of time.
The blast of death
Rang its bells in the hearts of the homes.
The grim face in the mirror
Faded with time into the slag heaps
From where he came.
The moon revealed its ugly village casa.
A dog howled its death-like sound,
A baby cried from the cold of the night,
A father knelt in
the bowels of the earth, waiting for light
In darkest hell, where he never saw.
Only winter remained.
And nothing returned to the nest
In the tree, but the snow that covered
The world of his past.

Roque Dalton

Headaches

It is beautiful to be a Communist,
although it brings on many a headache.

You see, the headaches of Communists
are supposed to be historical, that's to say
they do not submit to analgesic pills
but only go with the achievement of an earthly paradise.
That's the way it is.

Under capitalism our heads ache
so they just take off our heads.
In the revolutionary struggle, the head is a time bomb.
In constructing socialism our headaches are pre-planned
which doesn't make it any better; on the contrary
Communism will be, among other things,
an aspirin as huge as the sun.

Translated from Spanish

Gathering Lilac

She was always going somewhere...

Those last five years she died with me
were spent in gathering lilac.
I don't know who you are my dear,
but thanks a lot. How kind you've been.
I hope we'll meet again quite soon.
Then I'd be Mum and hold her tight,
and beg her stay a little while,
remind her how we used to sing
We'll Gather Lilac in the Spring

She was always going somewhere...

Those last five years she died with me
were spent in gathering lilac.
A policeman brought her back one day,
a naked mouse in an overcoat;
she spat and screamed and scratched at me
as if I'd sprung the trap that nailed her.
I took her by the hand and sang
the words she knew and loved so well,
she held me close, my Mum, until —

she was always going somewhere...

Those five last years she died with me
were spent in gathering lilac.
She'd pack her handbag furtively,
a comb, a photograph of Dad,
a twig cut from the lilac tree.
Put out the light! The warden's here!
Your father's legs are weeping shrapnel.

She was always going somewhere,
those last five years she died with me.
I don't know who you are my dear
but thanks a lot. How kind you've been.
I said *Goodnight, God bless you Mum.*
We'll Gather Lilac in the Spring.

Jeremy Kingston

Saving Face

I saw a dying soldier with no face.
Something had sliced it off like crust from a pie,
a raw meat pie, some teeth and a green eye
mysteriously still in place.
His best mate, vomiting, had the grace
to kill him — and who would not want to die,
a pulpy red mess, there to horrify
with its disfigured, agonized grimace.

I hear that somewhere safely overseas,
where copses shelter pretty things to hunt
in landscapes carefully designed to please
our leaders look for some face-saving stunt.
There'll be a banquet, lobster, caviar:
I'd make the bastards choke on steak tartare.

John Heath-Stubbs

A Love Charm

Hard as a quince, dreamy and decadent as a medlar,
Crisp as an apple, sweet and gritty like a pear —
A pear that is going sleepy,
Smooth and slippery as an eel, quick as a silverfish,
Prickly as a horse-chestnut in its case,
Or as a burr, or clinging goose-grass,
Singing and soaring, like a skylark,
Towards the cumuli, plummeting
Like a hawk to her prey, brash as a sparrow
Dust-bathing in the midst of the highroad,
Erratic as a dancing butterfly, committed
As a wood-ant foraging among the pine-needles,
Prompt as a taxi on call, or as the post,
Dodgy and unpredictable as a roulette wheel,
Dilatory as a summer afternoon
For punting or canoeing up the river,
Brisk as a September wind
With a touch of frost in it, drifting like thistledown,
Or like the soft fluff of rose-bay
Growing from earth that fire has ravaged,
Distant as a bright star, nearer than the jugular,
Haunting as a half-remembered dream,
Or a ghostly whiff of perfume, or the snatch of a tune —
All these I would have you be, and when these images
At last have been counted, have been discarded,
Fallible, wounded, human.

David Floyd

All gone to the Dogs

I've heard it's all gone to the dogs
but what have the dogs done to deserve it all?

In the Bible it says
that the meek will inherit the earth
not the dogs.

And where were the dogs
in the good old days?

Did they sit moping
on black and white street corners
waiting to get it?

Or did they take positive action:
incline their heads enticingly
slowly drawing it towards them
welcoming it with big, shiny teeth?

Now that the dogs have got it
is there any way we can ever
get it back?

Or are the dogs just too powerful?

Will they keep all of it forever
like a red sponge ball in their doggy mouths
chewing it, dropping it and
chewing it for eternity?

Murray Shelmerdine

Nothing Ever Stays the Same

there is a vulture called Caligula
sitting on the roof ridge
I thought perhaps he came
to eat the squirrels
or the crows
something should
but he ignores them
staring only at me
little flaming eyes
huge Roman nose
he's been driven mad by global warming
an illegal immigrant
who wants my house
and my liver
he plans to make his horse
chairman of Haringey Council
he might as well
I stayed indoors for three days
when I peeped out
I saw hyenas peeping in
through the brambles
cranes dabbing at the brassica
enormous insects inspecting the compost
I went to chase them away
Caligula's left eye impaled me
I scraped back inside
locked the door
drank whisky
ate a doughnut
I can hear strange noises out there
I think it's a rhinoceros
rubbing against the damson tree
I'm expecting the legions of wart hogs
and baboons very soon
I won't be able
to build the wall in time
I'll have to rely on diplomacy

Valerie Darville

In the Orange Grove

Yesterday they bulldozed the orange grove
when the boy, Mohammed, was fetching paint
in a bucket for his father. The troops
shot him in the head in the name of peace.
He lay among the crushed green branches.
Today the grandmother squats and sorts
oranges from among the broken leaves.
The father washes his son's blood with his
own tears, curses, calls down the wrath of Allah.
His brothers plot revenge. His sister prays,
proclaiming her brother is a martyr
in Paradise. The mother sits, slowly
turning his clothes over and over. Small
phantoms play about her, their voices echoing.
Unnoticed, an old woman sorts
oranges that her family may live.

Robert Ilson

Incidental Music for Collateral Damage

"They'll welcome us," the President said.
The generals said, "They'd better !
For we've got everything relevant planned
— Down to the wind and weather."

So after a bit of shock and awe
And a surge or two the soldiers
Sashayed along the conquered streets
Engaged on looking bolder.

And everywhere they marched they heard
A cackling crackling clatter
That might have been the crowds' applause
— Or the Kalashnikovs' chatter.

And when they got back to their barracks they found
They were missing a lad or two
Who'd got delayed by a classy dame
Whose name is Death to you.

And that's not counting the locals who
Went off with that same lady
Because of an inappropriate noise
Or a look or a gesture maybe.

And it's been that way since year one and some
Would have it go on for ever
With guns and drums and severed thumbs
So the Powers That Be look clever.

But them and all their bloody crew
Bear the invadees' curse:
However bad it is today,
Tomorrow will be worse!

Jeremy Kingston

Being Pius

Observe Pope Pius, scraping Jews
like shitballs off his neat white shoes;
the gold for his pince-nez he took
from a girl's jaw in Ravensbruck;
but now his pale eyes brim with pity
for the art-works in the Eternal City:
daily he offers prayers for them
at a statue of the B.V.M.
carved in white wood from Bethlehem.

Mary's a Jewess he'll accept,
he weeps remembering how she wept
to watch her son die on the tree
more slowly than with Zyklon-B.
We are naïve to be surprised
Pope John Paul wished him canonized.
— Deep in the Pit Pope Pius flits.
Now John Paul joins him there and sits
smirking with the hypocrites.

Frida Knight

Hymn to Friendship
(to a melody by Mozart)

Let us now by friendship guided,
By no creed or race divided,
Sing of peace,
Our right from birth.
As good-will and friendship bind us,
Thoughts of ill left far behind us,
Be it so over all the earth,
Be it so over all the earth.

Pray that strife and sorrows perish,
Render thanks for joys we cherish,
Which from Nature's bounty flow.
May these blessings be extended
To all people and never ended.
So may health, grace, goodness flow
So may health, grace, goodness flow.

Honour, truth and justice ever,
Wisdom love and high endeavour
Be our duty and delight.
East to West, each human being
Live in peace and plenty seeing.
Friendship fair and heavenly light,
Friendship fair and heavenly light.

Paul Birtill

Mid-Life Crisis

"But doctor, look at my hands,
just look at them, they're all wrinkled."
"Well you're nearly fifty. What do you expect?"
was the unsympathetic reply.
"But I haven't lived! I haven't bloody lived"
he exclaimed, tears rolling down his face.
"Well that's not my fault. Would you like
a prescription for some hand cream or perhaps
an anti-depressant?"

Anthony Fisher

Go Polish Your Bugle
(after 'Tommy' by Rudyard Kipling). '

Go polish your bugle
please bang your drum.
We have no bullets
to put in your gun.

You'll be smart and march,
drill with precision.
Never mind that there's
no ammunition.

Your gun, it will jam
but please wipe it still.
It needs to be clean
when they come for the kill.

They'll pinch your pension
deny that you're ill,
bully, torment you,
expect heroes still.

Church fathers will grab you
pious words for their god,
they'll not go to war
that's for you — poor sod.

Politicians'll tell you
that all is OK
and those that did wrong
stay hidden away.

We'll polish bugles
bang sombre drums,
regret that we had
no bullets for your gun.

Jane Elder

Old Man Reading
(based on a lithograph by Odilon Redon)

An old man reading in a darkened room —
the light streams in through thick encircled panes
and falls upon the pages of his book
on his bald forehead and his thick white beard.
His fingers trace the words, his face is calm
as if he read what gives him peace of mind.
His eyes are dark and watchful — what surprises
can he be hoping for, now, at his age?
Before him on the table other books
and burnt out candles catch their share of light.
The room is bare, save for his throne-like chair
and massive table where he props his tome.
He could be a magician or a sage
or pious reader of religious wisdom.
Does that face hold a touch of mischief in it
or is it wholly given up to learning —
serious, serene and ageless? Does he read
the history of his life, hidden till now
when he can find the thread that makes the sense
to trace the path out of the tangled web
the sunbeams seem to weave in the dark room?
No clock ticks there, only his breathing stirs
the silence of the dusty atmosphere —
the regular turning of the page once read
all the event he hopes for, all excitement.
 Still as an hourglass when the sands have settled
he waits and reads there in the darkened room
and still the light streams in, ever, for ever.

Paul Birtill

Benefit King

When I grow up I'm going to be
an astronaut a footballer a physicist
or be long term unemployed.

When I grow up I'm going to be
a rock star an actor a politician
or be long term unemployed.

When I grow up I'm going to be
a doctor a lawyer a fireman
or be long term unemployed.

When I grow up I'm going to be
an architect a marine biologist a painter
or be long term unemployed.

When I grow up I'm going to climb
Mt Everest invent things run my own business
or be long term unemployed.

When I grow up I'm going to have a beautiful wife
three lovely children a big house a flash car
or be long term unemployed.

Christopher Twigg

Listening To My Mother

I get moved
listening to my mother —
sitting outside
in the garden at Hinchley Cottage —
in folding summer chairs —
and she remembers
how she loved
summer evenings as a girl
when she was in bed and heard
her parents' voices in the garden —
"I just used to love hearing them" she says
and I am moved and try not to show it
and she is moved and shows it a little —
"they'd have gone out after supper" —
"What would they be doing?" I ask.
"Oh, they'd be looking at things" —
the purple irises among the high green grass
by the plastic bag with the compost —
the Needham's orchard beyond —
a spotted flycatcher nesting precariously
upon the garage rafter —
things I only started to notice properly
since I was ill —
that golden thread which as Machado says
links memories to soul —
I rejoice in the tears and the sorrow
for I know my life is real —
my losses are real, my body is real,
my hymns and hands are real —
I feel their passing wisdom —
the voices of my dead
grandparents in the garden.

Mario Petrucci

Directive I A
(Chernobyl, 1986)

those men
still warm from their beds
with the smell of their women
clinging to them — just like '37

bury them

the heads
of cabbage pulsing
thick veins
the turnip and carrot
the grain in its ears
the slim flowered dress
and wedding band

under white sand

that old woman sick
in her cot who rose
to meet the men in suits
yellow as devils yet
out she stepped
to raise her stick

bury her quick

the fireman in gumboots
his heelprint in fuel
lads ragged with rays
carrying the flag
straight into hell
each figure that is
a walking root
dripping gas and
speaking grit

all in plastic and into the ditch

the head of the commune
secretly rich the peasant
on all fours digging
with a spoon the bandit
the Major the clown
and buffoon

eight foot down

the milkchurn full of moonshine
that milkmaid spitting rust
the "we're going to the circus"
so her child will climb the truck

dig to the rock

the sparrow without branch
or byre the magpie and crow
seeking windshield and tyre
the chick in its nest only half
grown the grub the larva
the cat and the hound
the beetle the spider
still in its web the doe
and the vixen the wolf
and the roe the forest the
treetops the rivers and
air the mountains the
oceans the planets and
spheres the seasons the
cosmos the race to
the moon

make a sarkophágos —
bury them

soon

Valeria Melchioretto

Paul
(after Rainer Brambach)

As a child you chased the ball,
fled from local bullies,
fell and bruised your knees,
took play out of playground,
got up like a soldier and ran.

Twenty years on, you witness
soldiers shooting bullets
into clouds which stained
the bandaged sky crimson
but you kept running.

Then one night in old age,
having never been the same,
instead of falling asleep
you fell through that bullet-hole
in the floored sky and died.

Oh Paul, what would you say:
Hundred years gone, now
bullets stain playgrounds crimson,
bullies own the defeated sky
and mothers have nowhere to run.

John Heath-Stubbs

A Partridge in a Pear Tree

On the first day of Christmas, my true love sent to me...

A partridge perched on a pear-tree bough
On Christmas day — *une jolie perdriz*:
She had grown plump on stubble-gleaning
In September, and had dodged the guns.

Bare the branches now, but when spring comes
Leaves shall deck them and at summer's close
Depending pears, great tears of musky sweetness.

Alan Chambers

Three Christmas Riddles

Perdix, perdix
whose call is a rusty lock
that sticks,
in a jug you might find a flock,
but on the first day you will see
only one sits in this tree.
❄
Steady then, steady.
Was anything ready
in an oft repeated fable
of a birth that shook the Earth?
Now you should be able
to confirm the answer's firm.
❄
Two legs manic,
snapped shut.
Don't panic,
just mind your nut.

Katherine Gallagher

Circus-Apprentice

I'm learning it all — acrobatics, clowning,
riding bareback and trapeze,
fire from a sleeve: my hand's a wand.

I weave my life round dancing elephants
who spray the air while turning
their backs on the crowd;

lions who never put a foot wrong.
I'm taking their cue, I've seen
what people want.

Prancing ponies teach me steps:
pacing, adroitness, like my fellow-dancers
keeping their spot.

I'm walking the high-wire, making my mark
poised, balanced, don't look away —
you are my gravity's other edge.

Antonio Machado

My Poets

The first is called Gonzalo de Berceo,
Gonzalo de Berceo, poet and pilgrim
who on one of his journeys collapsed in a meadow
and who is always depicted copying a parchment

He rhymed at Santo Domingo, he rhymed at Santa María,
and at San Millán, at San Lorenzo and Santa Oria
and he said "my teaching it isn't something I've made up...
it comes from written sources... it's the truth"

His verse is sweet and solemn - monotonous threads
of winter poplars where nothing shines
lines like furrows in the brown fields
and far off the blue mountains of Castile

He tells us of the recovery of the exhausted pilgrim
reading from missals and in old prayer books
copying old histories he gives us his teaching
while all around him shines the light of his heart

Translation by Christopher Twigg

Robert Burns

Auld Lang Syne

Should old acquaintance be forgot
And never brought to mind?
Should auld acquaintance be forgot,
And auld lang syne!

For auld lang syne, my dear.
For auld lang syne,
We'll tak a cup o' kindness yet,
For auld lang syne.

And surely ye'll be your pint stowp!
And surely I'll be mine!
And we'll tak a cup o' kindness yet,
For auld lang syne.

We twa hae run about the braes,
And pou' the gowans fine;
But we've wander'd mony a weary fit,
Sin' auld lang syne.

We twa hae paidl'd in the burn,
Frae morning sun till dine;
But seas between us braid hae roar'd,
Sin' auld lang syne.

And there's a hand, my trusty fiere!
And gie's a hand o' thine!
And we'll tak a right gude willie waught,
For auld lang syne.

John Watkins

Has the Fire Really Gone Out?

His trousers fitted him once
Now they hang in bulk
Wrapped around a bony frame
Heavily belted at the waist.

The slow awkward shuffle
Definite and determined
To get there and back.

In the supermarket he pushes
A trolley up and down
The aisles, full of food
He cannot eat.
A list in his hand
Measures today's progress.

On the way home
He stops at the off-licence
And buys a miniature
To prove he still has the bottle.

Anthony Edkins

The Importance of Libraries

When I finish reading a book
I have a sense of achievement.

It's as if I were the author
pleased to have solved problems of style
content and communication.
(Audiences clap performers
because latter flatter former
by making them more self-aware)
But there are different degrees.
Sometimes achievement reaches art;
words like catharsis, charisma
come to mind, flattering reader:
I need to have books close to hand
to reread and refer to —
and as a constant reminder
of continuing achievement.

Mario Petrucci

Fish Stew
(Chernobyl, 1986)

Look. Here is a maid
milking. Observe. The Counter

by the teat of the cow
gives no sound. This bowl

of fish stew. Bought moments
ago from an open-air kiosk.

Not a click. These babies
pink as piglets squirming

in the sand. Note the twigs —
the stones in their mouths.

Do they cry? This woman
shrunk in bed to the size

of a child. That infant
whose blood separates

like soup. Nothing. Nothing
at all. Here is a family who

smelled the smoke. Do
the graves make a murmur?

And here. A man chewing
soft fuel from the reactor —

watch how his eyes spark
like firecrackers. Yet

the Geigers in his mouth
and rectum barely register.

Look. You can see
for yourselves. See

how rumours are
dangerous. This

is a fact.

Andy Croft

In the Brecht Museum
for Karen Leader

Look over there — it's that famous flat cap,
And here are the glasses, a pair of old shoes,

This must be the chair where he worked on those elegies,
These are some paperbacks he never read,

And this is the bed where he suffered the heart-attack,
Here is the time-piece that stopped when he died,

The table is set as though friends are invited,
The bottle is corked and the food is still hot,

In the desk is a poem he never got round to,
That list of suggestions that nobody followed,

And there on the mantelpiece, still in the ashtray,
A half-smoked cigar, the tobacco still burning,

And here by the fire is an unfinished argument,
These are the masks that he liked to put on,

On the wall by the door is a gesture of loyalty,
Here in a drawer is the private despair,

And here is the patience and there is the certainty,
These are the hopes and the unspoken doubts.

Outside the old garden is frozen in moonlight,
In a country that doesn't exist any more,

And over the border's a world that's still waiting
For the sun to come up and the future begin.

Dinah Livingstone

Focus

Some days I go about London
in a prosodic trance,
not listening to the meanings
of what people are saying,
just to the sounds and rhythms of their speech.
Oh! what bliss: 's' is a groovy fricative,
and that builder just called to his mate
in trochaic tetrameter catalectic,
might have said:
'Pass the bucket will you now,'
but I wasn't paying attention.
Now comes a true tetrameter,
the full eight syllables, perhaps it was:
'Got a tenner on the favourite.'

Later I remember
today is the Cheltenham Cup.
Subliminally I must have absorbed
more than his prosody. Oh! builder,
in your jaunty yellow hard hat,
balancing so graceful along that plank,
who speak the tongue that Shakespeare spake,
when 'thou thy worldly task hast done'
(trochaic tetrameter catalectic — Cymbeline),
did you knock off early
to watch the race in the pub
with your companions? I never checked
whether the favourite came in first.
I hope it did and won you a few quid.

That concentrated focus on prosody
brings moments of sheer heaven
but if I did it all the time
(some people think I do it quite enough),
without being anywhere aware
that that's not all that's going on,
I would be barmy.

Likewise you reductionist postmodernist,
who say there's nothing but language

or brain scientist interested only
in the brain's activities, yes, everything
can be considered under that one aspect,
for yes, that's your professional delight
(oh no, not here we go again:
that was an iambic pentameter),
maybe even necessary to do your job —
you too must have your wits about you
not to fall off your plank —
but if either of you seriously avers
that's ever all there is,
if the one discounts the mortal body
or the other ignores love and poetry,
isn't that blinkered vision also daft?

Robert Mitchell

Remembering Michael O'Riordan

Drinking a pint in the Waterloo,
Joking about Thomas Aquinas.
How many angels could you drown
In a pint of Guinness stout?
Picketing the American Embassy
Playing games with the photographer
At the window. There will be a laugh
In the CIA archives, thanks to Mick.
Browsing in the bookshop,
Pick a book at random off the shelf,
"Is this any good Mick?"
"Well he has a point to make,
But it's not a very good one!"
When does he get the time?
Not just the books he reads
But the ones he writes or edits as well.

I see a line of trenches stretching
Over arid hills. Young men
In leather coats with earnest
Faces. This is not a soldiers' war.
Soldiers respect their common avocation.
This is a war of utter hate!
Oh, they share the cigarettes
Drink wine and joke of girls.
(Probably the others do the same)
But there is no common ground with
Nazis, Fascists, Falangists,
Franco's Moors, the Condor Legion
Or the sharpest hate of all, the Blueshirts!

Mick, you were there and brought it
Home to us in that great book
That tells all time to come
That when "The workers of all the world
Stand on our guard on Huesca's plain,"
We Irish are not found wanting.

Ross Bradshaw

Learning Irish

I'm not sure what led me to be here
In the middle of a dance floor
Round a table set for nine.
Instead of plates
We have simple sentences, childish cartoons,
Difficult words to get our tongues round.

There are no letters for "x" and "z" in this alphabet.
I want to ask: How do you mark the spot
Where treasure can be found? What do bees do?

Downstairs the big fishing club
Is hard at it. Today is Wednesday.

For me it was always politics, politics.
And all those names...
Paisley and Stone, Sands and Tone,
The rhyme of a playground game.

But working now at this keyboard,
I can only be positive.
There's something about the accent over the letter "i"
That stops me translating "not".

And I can be many things I perhaps was once,
Perhaps could become.
For now living only in the present:

Is gasúr mé
Tá mé óg
Is athair mé
Tá mé mór
Tá mé an-go maith

I am a boy
I am young
I am a father
I am big
I am very well

Valerie Darville

Quotation from Byron

Reverently she smoothes
the creases of the silver gloves,
almost the length of her small arms.

(Bestowed upon her by an aunt —
no use to that doughty housewife —
"Where would I go to wear them?")

But the child fell under their spell.
Sparkling like diamonds
on her pearly pre-pubescent skin.

*She walks in beauty, like the night
Of cloudless climes and starry skies;
And all that's best of dark and bright
Meet in her aspect and her eyes.*

"Look at her! Who does she think she is!"
In shame she strips them from her hands
and hides the gift in her most secret place,

and boasts "I didn't like them really."
But within the woman, severely unadorned,
she walks in beauty.

Eve Pearce

Three o'clock in the Morning

I dreamed of you again
Federico Garcia Lorca.

As always a scent of roses
preceded your appearance
on a white horse, a garland round her neck,
her flanks drenched with sweat.

Federico Garcia Lorca
why do you come to me?

Can I stop the bullet in the field?

Your eyes when they look into mine
are bewildered — you were in a *safe* house,
the house of your friend — a Falangist —
but still a friend. His mother took you in.

The Black Squad came nonetheless —
oh yes, nonetheless

Federico Garcia Lorca —
your talent your undoing.

In the morning the sun shone,
the Alhambra sparkled
and they shot you 'with several others,'
buried you in the ravine where you fell.

You look into my almond eyes
with your round ones. Why do you come to me?

My heart leaps. Your white horse —
'Ah', the passion in that horse —
she rears and whinnies.

The scent of roses is overpowering.

Federico Garcia Lorca
I shall dream of you again.

Cathy Fodor

Wishful Thinking

Oh that my fingers were green
and of gardeners I could be queen,
but even my dahlias are horrible failures
and the grass isn't fit to be seen.
Why have all of my lupins gone gray
and my onions keep rotting away?
My poor little peppers are hiding like lepers,
they'll emerge and turn yellow one day.
Under stones crawl big fat wood-lice
indulging in plentiful vice;
the slugs and the snails are all wagging their tails.
My garden's a pests' paradise.

Dave Puller

Bombs R Us

We've got
Big bombs
Little bombs
Small bombs
Tiny bombs
Mini bombs
Thin bombs
Fat bombs
Dumb bombs
Loud bombs
Smart bombs
Quiet bombs
Cluster bombs
Round bombs
Long bombs
Square bombs
Flat bombs
Cheap bombs
Dear bombs
Lots of bombs
You want some
You're gonna get some

Adrian Green

Business Breakfast

On a blue September dawn
the tide ebbs under London Bridge.
We walk across — a crowd
alive but hypnotised.
So many left undead
for croissants and cappuccino.

And in the knowing,
unknowing,
and knowing again
of things we never
thought would matter,
breakfast sages
read our fortunes
in the coffee spoons,
project their fantasies
on office walls.

Later, on the Circle Line
the salesmen with their laptops
watch a couple sharing sushi
from a plastic box.

Racker Donnelly

Two for the Price of One

Shop
Till you Drop
is the New Jeru
salem. Jesus saves, and so can you!

Champagne, Shampoos,
Shammy-leather Shoes

TWO FOR THE PRICE OF ONE

Knock-kneed Chicken
that's finger-lickin'

TWO FOR THE PRICE OF ONE

Wonderbras! Canyons,
with Swell Companions.

TWO FOR THE PRICE OF ONE

Out in the Cold World, *God!*
Boo-hoo.
Labour and Tory: Peas in a Pod:

ONE FOR THE PRICE OF TWO

Notes on contributors

Dannie Abse is a Welsh poet and was a chest specialist. His most recent books are *New and Selected Poems* (Hutchinson, 2009) and *Two for Joy* a companion volume to *The Presence,* love poems for his late wife Joan. He still watches Cardiff City and plays chess. *The Appointment,*which appears in *Encounters* (Hearing Eye 2001), is a 'distorted mirror image of Bertolt Brecht's *Changing the Wheel* translated by Michael Hamburger'. **Page 24**

Timothy Adès is a translator-poet working mostly with rhyme and metre. His two books, Victor Hugo's *How to be a Grandfather* and Jean Cassou's *33 Sonnets of the Resistance*, are both represented in this anthology. His third book translates Jean Cassou again, *The Madness of Amadis*. **Pages 33, 60, 89.**

Rose Ausländer (1901-1988) was born in Austria-Hungary, emigrated to America in 1920, but returned in the 1930s; published her first book of poems in 1939; survived the war, first in the ghetto, then in hiding; eventually she settled in Germany and produced many more poetry collections. **Page 88.**

Andrew Bailey has worked for the Poetry Society, Poetry International Web and the Poetry Archive. Poems have appeared in several journals including *Stand, Brittle Star* and *Poetry Review*. He won the Geoffrey Dearmer Prize 2005, and was a contributing editor to *Lifemarks*, an anthology raising funds for the Motor Neurone Disease Association. His poem's dedication is to Peter Redgrove whose poetry 'is charged with a sense of wonder, mixing scientific and magical viewpoints', who died in 2003. **Page 90**

Wanda Barford was born in Milan during the Mussolini era. She emigrated with her parents to Southern Rhodesia (now Zimbabwe) where she spent many of her formative years. She then studied English at Southampton University and obtained her ARCM from the Royal College of Music. But in mid-life poetry took over entirely; she has five published collections. **Page 46**

Oliver Bernard was born in 1925, his parents an actress/singer and an architect. He left school at fifteen, joined RAF at seventeen, trained as a pilot, taught English and Drama, was a copywriter in Mayfair. He has published three collections of poems, two of poetry in translation (Apollinaire and Rimbaud), an autobiography *Getting Over It* and a CD, *Poems,* in 2008. **Page 69**

Paul Birtill was born in Walton, Liverpool in 1960. He moved to London in his early twenties and, except for a brief period in Glasgow, has lived there ever since. Several of his plays have been performed on the London fringe. **Pages 21, 40, 43, 54, 62, 74, 80, 85, 95, 106, 109.**

Ross Bradshaw runs Five Leaves Publications. He also organises Lowdham Book Festival and is Nottinghamshire County Council's Literature Officer. **Page 125.**

Alan Brownjohn, born in 1931, has published 12 volumes of poetry including a *Collected Poems* in 2006 and four novels. He has been active in anti-war campaigns since the first March to Aldermaston in 1958, and was briefly a Labour councillor (in Wandsworth). **Pages 26, 48.**

John Brunner (1934-95), a well known science fiction author, was an active member of CND. *The H-bomb's Thunder,* written in 1958, is still sung on anti-nuclear demonstrations. The tune is from an old US union song *The Miners' Lifeguard.* **Page 93.**

Robert Burns (1759-1796), Scotland's best known poet. *Auld Lang Syne* is sung worldwide. **Page 117.**

Peter Campbell was born and raised in Scotland and has been living in London since 1973. He is a mental health system survivor and was a founder member of Survivors Speak Out and Survivors Poetry. He works as a freelance trainer and writer and supports Hendon FC. **Page 64.**

Jean Cassou (1897-1986) was a major cultural figure in France, a poet and writer on art and poetry. During the Nazi occupation of France, he joined the Resistance in Toulouse but was arrested in late 1941. Deprived of writing materials, he composed sonnets in his head while in a Vichy prison. They are translated by Timothy Adès as *33 Sonnets of the Resistance* (Arc Publications 2002). From 1949 to 1965 he was director of the National Museum of Modern Art of France. **Page 60.**

Paul Celan (1920-1970) was born Paul Antschel in Romania to German-speaking Jewish parents. In 1942 his parents were interned in a labour camp, where his mother was shot and his father was either was either shot or died of typhus. After the war, he adopted the pseudonym Celan and moved to Paris in 1948. He drowned himself in the Seine in 1970. **Page 85.**

Alan Chambers is a founder member of Pitshanger Poets and edits *Poetry Ealing.* He has translated plays from French and Spanish which have been performed in the UK and USA. His poetry titles include *Ordered Lines, A Gregarious Creature?* and *Present Position.* **Page 114.**

Arthur Clegg (1914-1994) was a political activist and campaigner, journalist, Marxist historian, economist, teacher and poet. He was Far Eastern advisor on the *Daily Worker* and later its Foreign Editor. He was also for some years poetry critic for the *Morning Star. Human* is from his collection *The Eildon Tree* (People's Publications 1990). **Page 52.**

Andy Croft has published seven books of poetry. He writes a monthly poetry column in the *Morning Star* and lives in Middlesborough. He co-edited *Red Sky at Night: an Anthology of British Socialist Poetry* (Five Leaves, 2003) with Adrian Mitchell. *In the Brecht Museum* was commissioned by the South Bank Centre, London, to mark the 50th anniversary of the death of Bertolt Brecht in 2006. **Page 121.**

Roque Dalton was an important Salvadorean poet, journalist and revolutionary. He was assassinated by his own side in 1975. **Page 96.**

Valerie Darville, together with Jane Elder and Anthony Fisher, was a founder of Salisbury House Poetry evenings in Enfield. **Pages 102, 126.**

Brian Docherty was born in Glasgow and lives in North London. He has been a civil servant, hospital storeman, market trader, creative writing tutor and lecturer. He has two collections, *Armchair Theatre* (1999) and *Desk with a View* (2008). **Page 60.**

Racker Donnelly is an Irishman from Sheffield, a former UK slam champion poet and borough councillor. He has been performing his humorous verses for a decade at folk, comedy and poetry clubs and festivals, mostly in Ireland and England. A 'Racker' is a folk poet. **Page 131.**

Maureen Duffy is a notable contemporary British poet, playwright and novelist. Among her works are a literary biography of Aphra Behn, and *The Erotic World of Faery* a book-length study of eroticism in faery fantasy literature. *Naming* is from *Touching the Sun: Poems in Memory of Adam Johnson by Some of his Friends,* edited by Leah Fritz. **Page 49.**

Beata Duncan has taught English Literature and creative writing to students from nine to ninety, worked in publishing and as a researcher. Her poems have appeared in magazines, national papers and a pamphlet *Apple Harvest* (2000), and been broadcast on BBC Radio 3 and 4. She lives in North London. **Page 16.**

Anthony Edkins was born in Cheshire in 1927; except for sojourns in Spain and the USA, he has lived in London since 1950 and taught in the Spanish Department of University College London from 1985 to 1999. He has published translations from Spanish and five collections of poems. **Pages 23, 119.**

Jane Elder was born on the Isle of Man and educated there, read Classics at Cambridge and taught Latin, Classical Greek, English Literature and creative writing in schools and adult education. Her translation of Seneca's tragedy *Thyestes* (MidNAG and Carcanet 1982) was broadcast on Radio 3. Hearing Eye published her *Nine Noh Plays and Other Poems* and *The Cedar Forest*. She lived in Enfield and ran poetry workshops and readings at Salisbury House there. **Page 108.**

June English was born in Kent, spent her early childhood in Yorkshire, travelled widely and, during her first marriage, lived for several years on Vancouver Island. She has published three books of poems, lives in Kent and nurtures many other writers of poetry. **Pages 47, 97.**

Harry Eyres is a poet, essayist and newspaper columnist. He writes the weekly 'Slow Lane' column in the *Weekend Financial Times*. His first poetry collection *Hotel Eliseo* (Hearing Eye) was praised by Vernon Scannell in the *Sunday*

Telegraph as "an enjoyable collection of consistent accomplishment". He lives in London. **Page 32.**

Anthony Fisher is an industrial chemist and a Fellow of the Royal Society of Chemistry. He has been writing poetry since 1998 and reads regularly at Salisbury House, Enfield. His pamphlet *The Reek of Alchemy* (2009) concerns science, industry and history in his home town Enfield, Middlesex. **Page 107.**

Shelah Florey wrote from a unique viewpoint, humorously and wisely. She was born in Somerset, but lived most of her life in London and began writing poems after retiring. This poem appeared in her collection *The Making of Casablanca* (1999). **Page 36.**

David Floyd is a left-handed vegetarian who was born in north London in 1980. He sometimes writes for the *Morning Star*. He is a co-editor of Brittle Star poetry magazine. His pamphlet *War in the Playground* was published by Hearing Eye in 2003. **Pages 17, 25, 58, 79, 84, 100.**

Cathy Fodor comes from a musical family — her daughter was one of the original punk rockers — but her own interests lie more towards literature. She began writing poetry early, despite discouragement from others, and is still writing sixty years later. Her interests range from poetry to divinity and philosophy. **Page 128.**

Lynn Foote has published widely in magazines and is working on a travel memoir about the North. She has lived in London and Tokyo and works in the English Language Centre, Kings College London. **Page 63.**

Erich Fried (1921-1988) fled to London after his father was murdered by the Gastapo following the Anschluss in Austria. He published several volumes of poetry — the best known is *100 Gedichte ohne Vaterland* (1978). **Page 72.**

Leah Fritz, before moving to London in 1985, was best known in the USA for her writings on the anti-war, civil rights and feminist movements. Four collections of her poetry have been published in the UK. The poem *Brecht* originally appeared in *Spiral Bound* (Hearing Eye 2000), in *Acumen* magazine and is in her collection *Going, Going ...* (bluechrome 2007). **Page 48.**

Jacqueline Gabbitas was born in Worksop, Nottinghamshire, and uses the dialect in some of her work. In 2007 she was shortlisted in the New Writing Ventures Awards. Her pamphlet, *Mid Lands* was published by Hearing Eye the same year. She was awarded a Hawthornden Fellowship for 2009 to complete her first collection. She teaches on poetry courses and is a co-editor of *Brittle Star* magazine. **Page 83.**

Katherine Gallagher is a widely published poet, Australian in origin, resident in North London since 1979. She has four full length collections and a book of translations from French. The most recent are *Tigers on the Silk Road* (2000), *Circus-Apprentice* (2006) where both poems printed here appear, and *New and Selected Poems* (2009), all from Arc Publications. **Pages 51, 115.**

Donald Gardner, London born, moved to Amsterdam in 1980. Recent books include *How to Get the Most out of your Jet Lag* (Ye Olde Font Shoppe, USA 2001), *The Glittering Sea* (Hearing Eye 2006) and his translations of Remco Campert's poetry *I Dreamed in the Cities at Night* (Arc 2007). He is a celebrated performer of his own work — in Amsterdam, London and New York. **Page 42.**

Raymond Geuss was born in Evansville, Indiana (USA) in 1946. Since 1971 his day job has been to teach at various universities in Germany, the US, and Britain (Cambridge, where he is now Professor of Philosophy). His most recent academic book is *Philosophy and Real Politics* (Princeton University Press 2008). **Page 31.**

Adrian Green lives in Southend, Essex, the county where he was born. He has degrees in arts and psychology and has published two pamphlet collections as well as poems and reviews in several magazines and anthologies. His first full length collection is *Chorus and Coda* (Littoral Press). **Page 130.**

Martin Green was educated at A.S. Neill's Summerhill School; his parents fought in the International Brigades in Spain. He lives in Cornwall and is an author, playwright and poet. **Pages 77, 86.**

Lucy Hamilton was born in Norfolk, her mother French and her father Liverpudlian. She lives in Kent and taught international students at Ashford School. She is an editor for *Long Poem Magazine.* **Page 66.**

James Harvey studied biology at UCL, concentrating on ecology. After leaving university, he took up poetry full time, with biology inspiring much of his poetry. He has poems in magazines and in the anthology *In the Company of Poets*. **Page 81.**

Geoffrey Hazard was born in 1934 in Hackney, East London. He was in the Young Communist League and Communist Party. In 1950s—70s he was published here and in the US in many poetry magazines, and read his own work on the BBC Third Programme and at Live New Departures. He still publishes, though less often. **Page 74.**

John Heath-Stubbs (1918-2006) was educated at Queen's College, Oxford, and published his first poems during the second world war. One of the best poets of his generation, he became totally blind by the age of 60, but retained an exceptional visual memory and could find 'my way happily round the streets where I live'. *Artorius*, acknowledged as his masterpiece, appeared in 1974, Carcanet published his *Collected Poems* in 1988. The poems in this anthology all appear in *Torriano Sequences* (Hearing Eye 1997). **Pages 50, 99, 114.**

Heinrich Heine (1797-1856) was a German poet. His progressive thinking led to his books being banned in 1835. He worked as a journalist in Paris, admired Napoleon, supported strikes by Silesian weavers, and corresponded with Karl Marx. **Page 89.**

Nazim Hikmet (1902-1963) 'A socialist, a humanist, a human rights activist, a love and lyric poet — he changed the course of Turkish poetry.' While in prison from 1938 to 1950 — for 'incitement to Communism' — he wrote poetry translations and letters. His poetry was banned in Turkey and he spent the rest of his life in exile. **Page 37**

Vincent Homolka, born 1943 in New York, has lived in Britain for 41 years. He speaks several languages, his favourites being Portuguese and Yiddish. He has worked as a freelance translator, among other things. His translations of Ausländer and Celan are from *Over the Water* an anthology by the Camden Mews Translators group. **Pages 85, 88.**

Victor Hugo (1802-85) wrote many novels, plays and volumes of magnificent poetry. One of France's greatest writers, some of his best work dates from his long exile in Guernsey and Jersey. *Penniless Children* is from *How to be a Grandfather (L'Art d'Etre Grandpère)*, translations by Timothy Adès. **Page 33.**

Robert Ilson is an Honorary Research Fellow of University College London, sometime Associate Director of its Survey of English Usage, and a writer, editor, language-teacher, and lexicographer doomed at last to wake a poet (as Samuel Johnson was "a poet doomed at last to wake a lexicographer"). **Pages 83, 103.**

Arthur Jacobs (1937-1994) was born in Glasgow, growing up in a traditional Jewish family. Much of his poetry springs from this Scottish and Jewish inheritance. He lived at various times in Israel, Scotland and Spain, as well as London. He was a gifted translator of modern Hebrew poetry. Two small books of his poems were published in his lifetime; he left many more unpublished poems which were gathered in *Collected Poems and Selected Translations* (Menard Press/Hearing Eye 1996). **Pages 13, 71.**

Miroslav Jancic (1935-2004), was a Bosnian writer — journalist, playwright, novelist and also a political figure. When civil war began in 1992 in Bosnia-Herzegovina he was in Ghana as the Ambassador of the Socialist Federal Republic of Yugoslavia. He returned to Sarajevo under siege but his anti-nationalism and cosmopolitan humanity were scorned by the warring nationalist parties and he became a refugee in London. There he had 'an attack of poetry', writing in English; Hearing Eye published *The Flying Bosnian* in 1996, *Singing Through the Town* in 2001, and *Home Bloody Home/ Dome Prokleti Dome*, parallel poems in English and Bosnian/Serbo-Croat, in 2005. **Page 18.**

Emily Johns is an artist whose images span poetry and politics; the interests were meshed in *Drawing Paradise on the 'Axis of Evil'* work resulting from her visit to Iran on an international peace delegation. She trained at Goldsmiths College but is committed to pictures.

Adam Johnson was born in Cheshire in 1965, moved to London in 1984, died of an AIDS related illness in May 1993. Of the poetic achievement left by Adam, John Heath-Stubbs said 'that it is a lasting one, I have little doubt'. Two pamphlets appeared in his lifetime, *In the Garden* (1986) and *Poems* (Hearing Eye 1991), and two books posthumously, *The Spiral Staircase* (Acumen 1993) and *The Playground Bell* (Carcanet 1994). **Page 20.**

Jennifer Johnson was born in Bakht-er-Ruda in the Sudan, and she has worked as an agriculturalist in Zambia. She now lives in London, works as a copy editor and runs The Spinning Room poetry group and Nettle Press. Poems from the pamphlet *Footprints on Africa and Beyond* (Hearing Eye 2006) have been broadcast on Resonance FM. **Page 28.**

Johannes Kerkhoven, born in Holland, lived in Australia, now lives in London. His short stories and poetry have appeared in magazines and anthologies. In 2006 Hearing Eye published his collection of 'visual poetry' *Mixed Concrete.* He is also a graphic artist. **Pages 27, 39.**

Mimi Khalvati was born in Tehran and grew up on the Isle of Wight. She has worked as an actor and director in the UK and Iran and is the founder of The Poetry School. She has published 6 collections with Carcanet. *Come Close,* printed here, is an earlier version of the poem that appears in the most recent collection *The Meanest Flower,* which was a Poetry Book Society recommendation and shortlisted for the T.S. Eliot prize. **Page 40.**

Jeremy Kingston was born in London and lives there. Two of his stage plays have been produced in the West End and three on the Fringe. For the past twenty years he has been a theatre critic on *The Times.* His first poetry collection is *On the Lookout* (Hearing Eye 2008). **Pages 73, 87, 98, 104.**

Frida Knight drove an ambulance to Spain in 1937 and helped to look after refugee children. She made broadcasts from Madrid describing the bombing of civilians. Like many people who were involved with the Republican cause in Spain, Frida remained politically active all her life. She never gave up the hope that it is possible to build a better society 'even if it takes 100 years'. **Page 105.**

Bernard Kops was born in 1926 in the East End of London of Dutch-Jewish working-class parents. As well as poetry and novels, he has written more than 40 plays for stage and radio, achieving recognition with the first, *The Hamlet of Stepney Green.* **Pages 67, 75.**

Sarah Lawson was born in Indianapolis in 1943, but has lived in London since 1969. She has taught English Literature at Suzhou University in China; *All the Tea in China* recounts her experiences there in witty poems. She translates from French, Spanish and Dutch. She is an active member of International PEN. **Pages 18, 22, 14.**

Eddie Linden was born in Northern Ireland, grew up in Scotland, and lives in London. He is the founder editor of *Aquarius* literary magazine. His poems have been translated into French and Spanish and he has given readings in many countries. **Pages 62, 95.**

Dinah Livingstone is a poet and also a translator from various languages; her translations include *Zapatista Stories* by Subcomandante Marcos and *Poets of the Nicaraguan Revolution.* She lives in, and has run Katabasis Press from, the same house in Camden Town since 1966. *Focus* is from *Kindness* (Katabasis 2007). *May Day,* from her collection of the same title (1997), was written in response to Margaret Thatcher's attempt to abolish May Day. **Pages 82, 122.**

Ewan MacColl (1915-1989) folksinger and actor joined the Young Communist League at 14. One of his best-known songs, "The Manchester Rambler," was written after the pivotal mass trespass of Kinder Scout. In 1946 he and others formed the Theatre Workshop. **Page 94.**

Richard McKane is a poet and translator especially from Russian and Turkish. For many years he was an interpretor at the Medical Foundation for the Care of Victims of Torture. The translation of Nazim Hikmet's poems are included in *Poet for Poet,* his large volume of translations from Russian, Turkish and other languages and also his own poems. **Page 37.**

Antonio Machado (1875-1939), Spain's greatest twentieth century poet, was also a translator and playwright. He was born in Seville and died in Collioure in France as Spain fell to Franco. **Page 116.**

Liam Maguire, who died in 2006, was a published poet for four decades and a humanitarian for even longer. Politicised by his slum upbringing in Dublin, he was the least pompous and most playful of men who managed to be compassionate without being sentimental, and satirical without being cruel. **Page 78.**

Gerda Mayer was born in Karlsbad, Czechoslovakia and came to England in the Kindertransport in 1939 at the age of eleven. *Unseen* has appeared in several publications and is the epigraph to *Prague Winter,* autobiographical prose vignettes of childhood (Hearing Eye, 2005). **Page 34.**

Valeria Melchioretto was born in the German-speaking part of Switzerland; Italian is her mother's mother tongue. The UK has been her home since the early 90s. Her published books are Podding Peas (Hearing Eye 2004) and The End of Limbo (Salt 2007). She won a New Writing Ventures award in 2005. She is also a visual artist. **Page 113.**

Adrian Mitchell, poet, novelist and playwright was born in 1932 in North London and died in December 2008. He was one of the foremost poets of the anti-bomb movement. Kenneth Tynan called him 'the British Mayakovsky', Mitchell was for many years poetry editor of the *New Statesman.* His best known poem *Tell Me Lies* is the title of the posthumous collection, published by Bloodaxe, which contains these two poems which first appeared in the *Morning Star.* **Pages 55, 59.**

Robert Mitchell is a Morning Star reader who sent in the poem *Remembering Michael O'Riordan.* Michael O'Riordan was an active member of the Communist Party of Ireland and also fought with the Connolly Column in the International Brigades during the Spanish civil war. **Page 124.**

Eve Pearce is an actress. Born in Aberdeen, she came to London at twelve, fell in love with it instantly, and remains so. She regards herself as a Scottish Londoner. She has had one pamphlet published: *Woman in Winter* (Hearing Eye). She loves dancing, and is a member of the Company of Elders at Sadlers Wells. **Pages 45, 127.**

Perse Peett worked as a schoolteacher and as a puppeteer after having a very varied career including restoration stonemason. He now spends his time telling traditional stories with music and singing folksongs. **Page 19.**

Mario Petrucci is a physicist, ecologist, songwriter, educator and poet who creates a dialogue between science and poetry. He was the Imperial War Museum's first poet in residence. The poems printed here come from *Heavy Water: a poem for Chernobyl* (Enitharmon, 2004). **Pages 111, 120.**

Peter Phillips says 'Chocolate: it gets me into trouble. Well, I'm not in jail now. My wife has told me to be very careful what I eat and write, but I am still tempted.' His latest collection (2005) is *Wide Skies, Salt and Best Bitter*. **Page 41.**

Jacques Prévert (1900-1977) was a popular French poet, surrealist and screeen writer. His films include *Les Enfants du Paradis* and *Le Jour se Lève*. His first book was *Paroles* (1946). His poems are well known in France and widely taught in schools despite his antipathy to educational institutions. **Pages 14, 22.**

Dave Puller lives in Wythenshawe, Manchester. He is a writer, poet and left-wing satirical performer. *Bombs R Us* comes from the collection *Ouch* (Sorted Press). **Page 129.**

Jo Roach was born and brought up in London where she still lives, her father was from Ireland. She runs Pedal Power, an East London cycling club for learning disabled people. Her poetry is made from the ordinary and commonplace of everyday life. Her poems have been published in magazines in the UK, USA and Ireland, she has a pamphlet *Dancing at the Crossroads* (Hearing Eye) and her work was included in *Oxford Poets 2007: an Anthology* (Carcanet). **Page 30.**

Anna Robinson's first publication was *Songs from the Flats* (Hearing Eye); set on a housing estate in south London, it explores themes of home and rebellion within an urban dream-time. This was selected by the Poetry Book Society as their Pamphlet Choice in Winter 2005/6. Anna also featured in *Oxford Poets 2007* (Carcanet), *In the Company of Poets* (Hearing Eye) and *Entering the Tapestry* (Enitharmon). **Page 15.**

Jude Rosen is an urban cultural researcher and writer. Her poems have been published in the anthology *This Little Stretch of Life* and in her pamphlet *A Small Gateway* (Hearing Eye 2009). She is writing a long poem of walks, narratives and voices from the Lower Lea Valley and East End. **Page 53.**

Murray Shelmerdine lives in a wood in London. He presents 'Poetry Now and Then' on Resonance FM (www.resonancefm.com), London's arts radio station. His pamphlet *Sermons of Sedition* is out from Nettle Press; he is working on translations of the poems of Jules Supervielle. **Page 101.**

Janet Simon lives and sings in London. She has worked with homeless people and asylum seekers. She was a prizewinner in the National Poetry Competition. Her collection *Victoria Park* was published by Loxwood Stoneleigh. More recently her pamphlet *Asylum* was published by Hearing Eye. **Page 34.**

Hylda Sims has been a folksinger, teacher, communard, landlady and single parent. The child of itinerant communist market traders, she was educated at Summerhill, A.S. Neill's 'free' school, and was a founder member of The City Ramblers Skiffle Group. She runs poetry and music events. **Pages 44, 91.**

Gillian Spragg studied at the Guildhall School of Music and Drama, winning the coveted Gold Medal. She has been Director of the Kenya Conservatoire of Music. She is a composer, also teaches piano and performs both as poet and as pianist. **Page 56.**

Paul Summers was born in Blyth, Northumberland in 1967 and now lives in North Shields. **Page 57.**

Christopher Twigg was born in Worcestershire in 1958. He has published five collections of poetry, the most recent are *A Cherub that sees them* (Zenane 2003) and *The English Book* (Zenane 2005). He plays guitar for the alternative country group Chicken of the Woods and is a painter. **Pages 110, 116.**

John Watkins lives in Tredegar, South Wales. His collections are *Wheels, Come into the Warm* and *Stones*, from which these two poems are drawn. He is several times winner of the Dic Penderyn Essay Award at the South Wales Miners' Eisteddfod. **Page 118.**

Stephen Watts, poet, editor and translator, lives and works in Whitechapel in the East End of London; he has cultural roots in Scotland and in the Swiss Italian Alps. He has translated contemporary Persian poets, including Ziba Karbassi, and the Yiddish poet Avrom Stencl. His most recent poetry books are *The Blue Bag* and *Mountain Language/Lingua di Montagna* (with Italian translation by Cristina Viti). **Page 68.**